JORDAN
in Pictures

VGS

Jeffrey Zuehlke

Lerner Publications Company

Contents

Lerner Publishing Group realizes that current information and statistics quickly become out of date. To extend the usefulness of the Visual Geography Series, we developed www.vgsbooks.com, a website offering links to up-to-date information, as well as in-depth material, on a wide variety of subjects. All of the websites listed on www.vgsbooks.com have been carefully selected by researchers at Lerner Publishing Group. However, Lerner Publishing Group is not responsible for the accuracy or suitability of the material on any website other than <www.lernerbooks.com>. It is recommended that students using the Internet be supervised by a parent or teacher. Links on www.vgsbooks.com will be regularly reviewed and updated as needed.

Lerner Publications Company
A division of Lerner Publishing Group
241 First Avenue North
Minneapolis, MN 55401 U.S.A.

Website address: www.lernerbooks.com

web enhanced @ www.vgsbooks.com

Library of Congress Cataloging-in-Publication Data

Zuehlke, Jeffrey, 1968–
    Jordan in pictures / by Jeffrey Zuehlke.
        p. cm. – (Visual geography series)
    Includes bibliographical references and index.
    ISBN: 0-8225-1173-8 (lib. bdg. : alk. paper)
    1. Jordan–Pictorial works. 2. Jordan–Juvenile literature. I. Title. II. Series.
DS153.2.Z85 2005
956.95–dc22   2004020230

Manufactured in the United States of America
1 2 3 4 5 6 - BP - 10 09 08 07 06 05

INTRODUCTION

As an independent country, Jordan's history spans less than a century. Yet the history of the region that later became Jordan spans thousands of years and was the site of what may have been the world's first cities. A study of Jordan is not only a study of the modern Middle East but, in some ways, of civilization itself.

Lying in the very center of the Middle East, Jordan holds an unusual position in that troubled region. To the west, the country shares a long border with the embattled State of Israel and the Palestinian autonomous (self-ruled) territory of the West Bank. Jordan has been on the front line of the ongoing Arab-Israeli conflict for more than fifty years. To the east lies Iraq, which has been wracked with violence and instability since a U.S.-led coalition (group) of nations invaded the country in 2003 to remove Iraqi president Saddam Hussein. Syria, Jordan's neighbor to the north, has often expressed hostility toward Jordan—in particular toward Jordan's late ruler King Hussein and his moderate stance in regard to the Arab-Israeli conflict.

Tensions are also felt within Jordan itself. A significant portion of the country's population—perhaps as high as 60 percent—are Palestinian refugees who fled or were forced from their homes during the Arab-Israeli wars of the twentieth century. Most of these people live in crowded refugee camps and do not consider Jordan their true home. The Palestinian population has often been at odds with Jordan's leaders and with the native Jordanian population. Many Palestinians have wanted Jordan to take a harder stand against Israel. They also complain that native Jordanians treat them like second-class citizens.

Yet despite these pressures, Jordan has remained remarkably stable throughout its short history. Since declaring independence in 1923 (under the name Transjordan), the country has also progressed rapidly from being undeveloped with an uneducated population to being one of the Middle East's most modern and forward-thinking nations.

Much of the credit for this progress and stability has gone to one man, King Hussein, Jordan's monarch from 1953 to 1999. Throughout

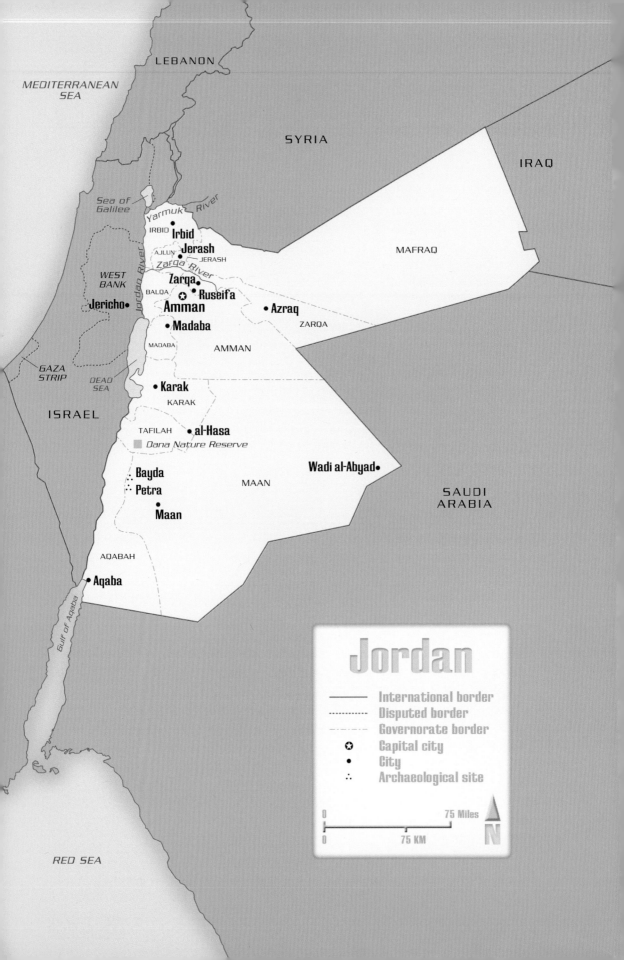

his forty-six-year reign, Hussein navigated his country through troubled waters with an uncanny combination of patience, decisiveness, and a willingness to compromise. Many of Hussein's actions were controversial. For example, he engaged in secret negotiations with Israel in the 1970s against the wishes of his own people and his Arab neighbors. But the king made his decisions based on what he felt was best for the long-term interests of his country. In most cases, history has shown Hussein chose the right course of action.

Hussein's successes in maintaining stability and promoting development are all the more remarkable given the country's financial situation. A small, poor, desert country with few valuable natural resources and only a small percentage of land suitable for farming, Jordan has depended on foreign aid throughout its history. Yet help from other countries has always had strings attached. Throughout his reign, Hussein was constantly forced to juggle the demands of foreign donors (Britain, the United States, and some of Jordan's Arab neighbors) with the demands and needs of his people.

When Hussein died of cancer in 1999, his son inherited the throne as King Abdullah II. Since taking power, Abdullah has followed in the footsteps of his father and has maintained Jordan as a moderate and stable state in a sometimes violent and troubled region. At the same time, Abdullah and the Jordanian government are pointing Jordan toward a bright future with an active program to make the country a hub for the Middle East's developing high-tech industry.

THE LAND

Jordan, whose full name is the Hashemite Kingdom of Jordan (Hashemite is the name of the kingdom's ruling family), is located in the Middle East. The country is bordered on the north by Syria, on the east by Iraq, and on the east and south by Saudi Arabia. To the west lie Israel and the West Bank, the Palestinian autonomous area that lies west of the Jordan River. Jordan controlled this area from 1950 until the Six-Day War in 1967, and until 1988 the nation continued to claim the area. Jordan proper, which lies east of the Jordan River, covers about 35,637 square miles (92,300 square kilometers) and is slightly smaller than the state of Indiana. Jordan's 16 miles (26 km) of coastline lie in the southwest on the Gulf of Aqaba, an arm of the Red Sea. The city of Aqaba, Jordan's only port, plays a large part in the economic life of the country.

◉ Topography

Jordan has three major geographical regions—the Jordan Rift Valley, the Jordanian Highlands, and the Jordan Desert. The Jordan Rift Valley

forms the border between Jordan and Israel and Jordan and the West Bank. About 1,300 feet (400 meters) below sea level at the Dead Sea, the Jordan Rift Valley contains the lowest point on the earth. Formed a million or more years ago by an earthquake, this deep depression is part of the Great Rift Valley, which extends from northern Syria to Mozambique in southeastern Africa. Within Jordan, the Jordan River flows through the northern half of the valley. South of the Dead Sea, however, the valley is known as Wadi al-Araba, and its elevation rises gradually to about 900 feet (274 m) above sea level.

With an altitude of between 2,000 and 5,000 feet (600 to 1,500 m), the Jordanian Highlands run parallel to the Jordan Rift Valley across the length of the country. Chalk, sand, limestone, and flint break through the soil in the highlands. South of Maan, volcanic rocks predominate, and the land is more mountainous. Mount Ramm, the highest point in Jordan at 5,689 feet (1,734 m), is located in the south. Wadis, or valleys that are dry most of the year, cut deeply through the highlands.

The Jordan Desert, part of the Syrian Desert, covers 82 percent of the country, with only occasional oases—fertile areas where crops can grow. The northern section of the desert is composed of hardened lava and basalt (a dark volcanic rock), and the southern part is made of sandstone and granite, partly eroded by wind. The two types of desert meet near the town of Azraq.

◎ Bodies of Water

The Jordan River, from which the nation takes its name, marks part of the frontier between Israel and Jordan, from the Sea of Galilee (also known as Lake Tiberias) to the Dead Sea. The waterway wanders for about 200 miles (322 km), draining the waters of the Sea of Galilee, the Yarmuk River, and the surrounding streams before finally flowing into the Dead Sea. Actually a lake, the Dead Sea is 45 miles (72 km) long and 10 miles (16 km) wide, but its waters are ten times saltier than the ocean.

THE DEAD SEA

Most geologists believe an earthquake created the Great Rift Valley about one million years ago. The Dead Sea sank into the valley and lost its natural outflow to the sea. The lake receives little rainfall, about 2.7 inches (7 centimeters) per year. The lake gets most of its water from the Jordan River. But this water quickly evaporates in the hot climate, causing salts to build up in the water and in the lake bed. The salt concentration in the water of the Dead Sea is about 33 percent, compared to 3 percent for the nearby Mediterranean Sea.

The Dead Sea's water is so saturated with salt and other minerals that virtually nothing can sink in it. In the first century A.D., future Roman emperor Vespasian tested this fact. He ordered people who couldn't swim to be thrown in the sea with their hands tied behind their backs. Even in deep water, they bobbed easily to the surface.

A woman floats effortlessly on the surface of the salty Dead Sea.

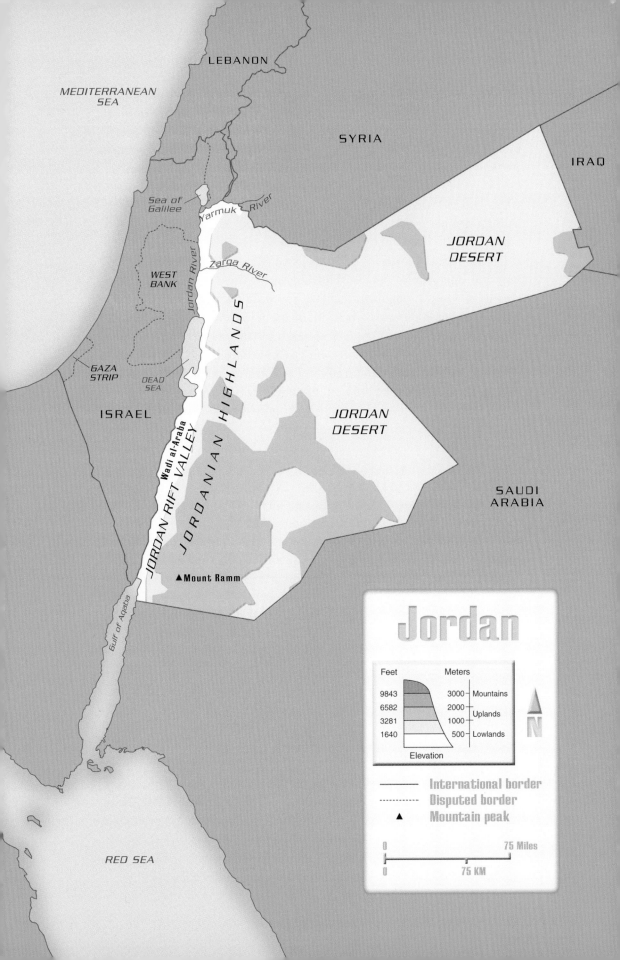

LEBANON

MEDITERRANEAN
SEA

SYRIA

IRAQ

Sea of
Galilee

Yarmuk   River

JORDAN
DESERT

Zarqa River

WEST
BANK

Jordan River

GAZA
STRIP

DEAD
SEA

ISRAEL

JORDAN
DESERT

Wadi al-Araba

JORDAN RIFT VALLEY

JORDANIAN HIGHLANDS

SAUDI
ARABIA

▲Mount Ramm

Gulf of Aqaba

Jordan

Feet	Meters
	3000 — Mountains
9843	
6582	2000 — Uplands
3281	1000
1640	500 — Lowlands

Elevation

N

——————— International border

- - - - - - - Disputed border

▲ Mountain peak

0   75 Miles

0   75 KM

RED SEA

The waters of the Jordan River are valuable for irrigation. Despite past attempts to create a plan to irrigate the entire valley, conflicts between the Arabs and the Israelis have at times hindered development. As a result, the nations bordering the river—Jordan, Israel, Syria, and Lebanon—have developed their own individual schemes for using the water. In doing so, they often deprive neighboring countries. The 1994 Jordan-Israel Peace Treaty included an agreement on sharing water and has allowed for an increase in Jordan's water resources.

Jordan has a number of water use programs in the planning, building, and operational stages. The largest of these is the East Ghor Irrigation Project, begun in the 1950s, which diverts water from the Yarmuk River, a tributary (branch) of the Jordan River that is shared by Jordan and Syria, to irrigate about 30,000 acres (12,140 hectares) of Jordanian agricultural land. Jordan increasingly relies on water from the Yarmuk and the Zarqa—another tributary of the Jordan—to irrigate its fields. Other projects to supply water include desalinization plants (which turn saltwater into potable, or drinkable, water) and adding more wells for extracting more water from belowground water supplies.

Climate

The climate of Jordan is generally arid (dry), varying from pleasantly mild weather in the Jordanian Highlands to harsh desert conditions in the east. The dry season between April and October is warm and sunny with cool evenings. Daily temperatures in the capital city of Amman in northern Jordan range from 53°F (12°C) in January to 90°F (32°C) in August. The contrast is even greater in the desert, where summer temperatures during the hottest part of the day occasionally reach 120°F (49°C), but bitter cold spells occur during the winter.

The amount of rainfall decreases farther inland, and the desert receives less than 5 inches (13 cm) of annual precipitation, while the highlands receive 20 inches (51 cm) or more in the north and 12 inches (30 cm) in the south. Rainfall varies greatly from year to year throughout the country, which complicates agricultural planning.

The country as a whole is often prey to extended droughts. When it does rain, most of the precipitation falls during the cool winter months from November to March. In all regions, except the Jordan Rift Valley, frost—and sometimes snow—is fairly common. For about a month at the beginning and the end of the rainy season, hot dry air from the deserts to the south and southeast may produce strong winds called khamsins. Although these windstorms can cause much discomfort and destroy crops, they rarely last more than a day.

A field of **red poppies** blooms near the Dead Sea.

Flora and Fauna

Despite Jordan's location in the desert, flowers bloom throughout the land from February to May. Flowering plants found in Jordan include poppies, roses, irises, anemones, and wild cyclamens.

About 212,500 acres (86,000 hectares) of forest exist in Jordan, and most of the trees grow on the rocky highlands. Heavy woodcutting by villagers and extensive grazing by flocks of sheep have depleted some forested areas. But a reforestation program that the Jordanian government began in 1948 has partially restored some forests. Predominant types of vegetation reflect the amount of rainfall. Evergreen oaks and Aleppo pines thrive where rainfall is heaviest. Grass and shrubs cover the semidry plateaus, and thorns and sparse shrubs survive in the desert. Olive trees grow wild in many places.

The wildlife of Jordan includes more than 70 species of mammals—both African and Asian—including jackals, hyenas, foxes, and mongooses. Wild boars and ibex (wild goats) roam the desert. Until fairly recent times, lions and leopards stalked their prey on Jordanian soil, but these great cats are extinct there. A curious creature is the hyrax, a small, rabbitlike animal that can climb with its hooflike claws.

Birds—including golden eagles, vultures, pigeons, and partridges—are numerous, with an estimated 350 different species. Because of the dry climate, water-loving animals are few, but reptiles abound with at

The **ibex,** a species of mountain goat, and the **golden eagle** are two of the many species of wildlife found in Jordan's varied landscape.

least 73 different species counted, including many kinds of snakes and lizards. Insects and their kin, such as locusts (grasshopper-like bugs)—which have attacked crops for centuries—thrive in the dry regions.

Natural Resources and Environmental Concerns

Unlike its neighbors Saudi Arabia and Iraq (the world's two biggest oil-producing nations), Jordan has virtually no oil resources to exploit. The country has just two small oil wells. Jordan's main natural resources are phosphate and potash—both of which are used to make fertilizer. Although Jordan mines these minerals in abundance, they are not nearly as profitable as crude oil. Jordan does, however, have large reserves of oil shale—rock from which oil can be extracted. The Jordanian government is pursuing opportunities to make the country a top oil shale producer.

Like most Middle Eastern countries, Jordan's main environmental concerns are related to a lack of water resources. The country's arid environment has not been able to keep up with the country's rapid population increase over the past several decades. Desertification (a process in which land previously suitable for farming turns to barren desert due to mismanagement), deforestation, and overgrazing have all taken their toll on Jordan's environment. In 1991 the Jordanian government formed a Department of the Environment to implement programs that have helped to protect Jordan's land. These programs include educating the country's farmers in the most efficient and earth-friendly farming methods, limiting the reduction of forests, and setting aside parts of the country as nature preserves.

In the 2000s, Jordan's biggest environmental challenge involves finding ways to provide sustainable amounts of water for its citizens. The country needs more than 300 billion gallons (1.150 billion cubic meters) of water each year for home, industrial, and agricultural use but has access to only 225 billion gallons (850 million cubic meters) of renewable water. The Jordanian government has introduced a strict water-rationing program, allowing a per capita (per person) supply of 24 gallons (90 liters) per day—one of the lowest in the world. The government supplies a set amount of water every two weeks, and households are required to make their water supply last until the next ration is delivered.

Overuse of limited water resources is also threatening the Dead Sea, which is in danger of drying up completely. Jordanian, Israeli, and Syrian irrigation projects have all diverted the Jordan River's waters, greatly reducing its inflow to the Dead Sea. Jordan and Israel have discussed plans to build a canal from the Red Sea to carry water to the Dead Sea. The canal would also be used to generate hydroelectric power to run proposed desalinization plants for both countries.

⊚ Amman

Long before recorded history, people dwelt among the hills of Amman— the capital of Jordan—where they enjoyed the cool waters of the area's many springs. Modern Amman is a fast-growing commercial and cultural hub of the country. Its population has increased from 20,000 in 1920 to nearly 2 million in the 2000s. The city is a famous tourist attraction ,originally situated among seven hills but sprawling over nineteen in the twenty-first century.

DOWNTOWN AMMAN

"Downtown, small, dusty Palestinian boys ran about with wooden trays on their heads, piled high with bread and cakes, and old men sold Bedouin coffee from elaborate silver pots as they huddled in doorways with their makeshift wheeled stoves. Cafés curled with smoke from *narjileh* pipes, fat cracked from pans of felafel cooked at the roadside. Second-hand Western clothes were haggled over by men wearing a hundred variations on traditional Arab dress, while veiled women struggled to cross terrifyingly busy roads with armfuls of babies. Downtown never ceased to be a racket of shouts, traffic, music. . . . "

—Annie Caulfield (British writer), *Kingdom of the Film Stars: Journey into Jordan* (1997).

Before 1875 Amman was nothing more than the ruins of the once-prosperous Roman city of Philadelphia. When Circassian people immigrated to Jordan from the Caucasus region of southwestern Russia in the late nineteenth century, they settled in the area of Amman and are sometimes credited with having rebuilt the city. In 1929 Amman was declared the capital of the newly established, independent nation of Transjordan.

Because Amman is a newly rebuilt city, it lacks the ancient architecture of classical Arab capitals, such as Damascus, Syria, or Baghdad, Iraq. The most impressive ruin in Amman is a two-thousand-year-old Roman theater, which was built in three tiers into the semicircular curve of a hill. The theater seats six thousand spectators and is still used for outdoor drama festivals and orchestral concerts.

Few people who live in Amman claim that they are originally from the city. In fact, the majority of the population is Palestinian, many of whom made their way to the city as refugees following the several Arab-Israeli wars of the twentieth century. These influxes of refugees have forced the city to expand rapidly, creating severe shortages of housing and other community services. Nevertheless, development has exceeded expectations, and residents of Amman enjoy better facilities and employment opportunities than do many other Jordanians.

Secondary Cities

IRBID, located in the north, is Jordan's second largest city, with a population of 745,000. Nestled in the Jordanian Highlands, Irbid has been an

Amman, the capital city of Jordan, stretches across hills known as jabals. Each jabal defines a different neighborhood. For links to learn more about Jordan's cities, visit www. vgsbooks.com.

important agricultural center since ancient times. The city is home to Yarmuk University, which houses two of the country's best museums, the Museum of Jordanian Heritage and the Jordan Natural History Museum.

ZARQA, located just northeast of Amman, is Jordan's third largest city, with a population of 623,000. The city was founded in the nineteenth century by Circassians and later became a headquarters for the Arab Legion, Jordan's army. The major site for the nation's industrial development, Zarqa hosts an oil refinery and a tannery (leather-making factory) on its outskirts. The city is also the site of the oldest Palestinian refugee camp in the country. The Zarqa refugee camp is home to about 18,000 people and is one of four such camps established by the International Red Cross after the 1948 Arab-Israeli conflict.

AQABA (population 74,000), lying on the Red Sea's Gulf of Aqaba, is Jordan's only seaport. Set against a rugged background of stark mountains, the city features beaches and blue waters, which attract sun-loving tourists. Throughout its history, Aqaba has served as a crossroads connecting trade routes in Asia, the Middle East, and Europe, and the city's busy port remains a hub of economic activity.

Historic Cities

Jordan has numerous smaller communities, several of which are renowned for their archaeological sites. The largest and best known of

PETRA

"It is certainly one of the most wonderful scenes in the world. The eye wanders in amazement from the stupendous rampart of rocks, which surround the valley, to the porticos and ornamented doorways sculptured on the surface. The dark yawning entrances to the temples and tombs and the long ranges of excavated chambers, give an air of emptiness and desolation to the scene, which I cannot well describe. . . . "

—British traveler John Kinnear, 1839

these is the ancient city of Petra. Located in Jordan's rocky southwest, the city is set deep inside a narrow gorge and is half-built and half-carved into the rock. The area has been inhabited since prehistoric times. But many of the city's greatest landmarks were built by the Nabataeans, an industrious Arab trading people, as early as the third century B.C. Listed as a World Heritage Site by the United Nations Education, Scientific, and Cultural Organization (UNESCO), Petra is Jordan's most popular tourist attraction and brings in thousands of visitors each day.

Lying in northern Jordan, Jerash is recognized as the best and most completely preserved Greco-Roman city in southwestern Asia. In the second and third centuries A.D., Jerash thrived under Roman rule, but later the city fell into ruin. The Jordan Ministry of Tourism and Antiquities has restored several different areas, revealing hundreds of stately columns, a triumphal arch, and other splendid ruins.

Lying south of Jerash and Amman, Madaba dates from the middle Bronze Age (2100–1500 B.C.). The city is best known for its Byzantine mosaics (images made from tiny colored pieces of glass, tile, or gems) from the period of Eastern Roman rule. One of Madaba's treasures is a sixth-century A.D. mosaic map of Jerusalem, the oldest map of the city. It is embellished with pictures of monasteries, people, boats, and plants. Other fine mosaics from other parts of Jordan have been transferred to Madaba, where a museum displays depictions of Greek heroes and gods as well as exhibits of Roman jewels and utensils.

Karak Castle rests on a hill above the town of Karak. Built in 1132, Karak was strategically located on the caravan trade route between Egypt and Syria.

Farther south, in west central Jordan, lies the town of Karak, an outpost for Christian crusader armies during the twelfth century. The stronghold rests on the ancient trade routes that led from Arabia to Egypt and the Mediterranean. Robbing caravans laden with ivory, spices, metals, jewels, and richly decorated silks became a vital source of income for the military outposts of the Crusades. Karak's castle-fortress, one of the most famous in the Middle East, was built by the French crusader Godfrey of Bouillon.

HISTORY AND GOVERNMENT

The Hashemite Kingdom of Jordan is a twentieth-century creation. Its modern-day borders were drawn in the 1920s. But the land east of the Jordan River has a very long and rich history and is home to what may have been some of the world's first cities. Valued for its strategic position as a crossroads between Asia and Africa, Jordan has been invaded and controlled by many peoples over the last three thousand-plus years.

◐ Early History

Archaeologists have uncovered evidence that Jordan was once home to many Stone Age peoples. In the Jordan Desert, archaeologists have found chipped stone tools believed to be used by hunters living during the Paleolithic period (roughly 2,500,000 to 200,000 B.C.). By about 8000 B.C., inhabitants of the Jordan River valley had formed settlements at Bayda on the East Bank and at Jericho on the West Bank. These may have been history's first cities. Over the centuries, many

more settlements sprang up, and by about 3000 B.C., the area of the Jordan River valley was carrying on a brisk trade with Egypt.

In about 2000 B.C. came large numbers of Semitic-speaking peoples (the Semitic languages are early forms of many modern languages, including Arabic and Hebrew). Collectively known as the Amorites, they began to move southward, crossing the Euphrates River from northern Mesopotamia (northeastern Syria). These people gradually came to dominate the region, which they called Canaan.

Another Semitic people, the Israelites, had also lived in the region, but they left when a famine struck the land. The Israelites wandered into Egypt, where after a time, they were enslaved. In about the thirteenth century B.C., a religious prophet named Moses led them back into Canaan. For about two hundred years, the Israelites fought with the other peoples of Canaan for control of the region. Among their most powerful foes were the Philistines, who inhabited an area along the Mediterranean Coast called Philistia.

Three successive Israelite kings—Saul, David, and Solomon—managed to expand the kingdom of Israel to cover much of modern-day Israel and western Jordan. They developed Jerusalem as their religious and cultural center. Solomon's reign from 961 to 922 B.C. marked the peak of Israelite strength. After his death, the kingdom split into two domains—Israel in the north and Judah in the south. (The term Jew comes from the word Judah.)

The region's location on caravan and military routes made it strategically important over the next several centuries. During the eighth and seventh centuries B.C., invaders from the east—first, the Assyrians, followed by the Babylonians—conquered Israel and Judah. In turn, these empires were conquered by others—first the Persians (from about 531 B.C. to 331 B.C.), then the armies of the Macedonian king Alexander the Great.

While foreign armies invaded and occupied Jordan, an Arab people called the Nabataeans managed to hold off potential conquerors for generations. Although originally nomads, the Nabataeans constructed the secret stronghold of Petra in the cliffs of southern Jordan. Petra was carved out of the sandstone walls of a canyon that can only be reached by way of a narrow gorge between sixty-five-foot cliffs. But in the first century B.C., the Romans—an empire based in modern-day Italy—finally managed to conquer Petra, when Roman forces found the source of Petra's water and dammed it.

After conquering and occupying the area, the Romans named it Palaestina, after the old kingdom of Philistia. (The modern name

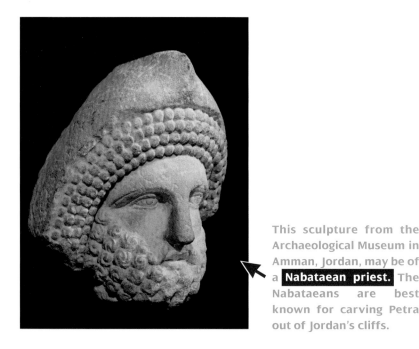

This sculpture from the Archaeological Museum in Amman, Jordan, may be of a **Nabataean priest.** The Nabataeans are best known for carving Petra out of Jordan's cliffs.

Palestine comes from the Roman Palaestina.) They installed Herod the Edomite as king of Judea, giving him power over all of the major Israelite tribes in the area.

During Herod's reign, the life of Jesus of Nazareth gave rise to the religion of Christianity. At first, Roman emperors harshly suppressed this new religion. (The Romans also expelled the Jews from the area in the second century A.D.) But as the centuries passed, Christianity became the accepted faith of the empire. The Roman emperor Constantine legalized the religion in A.D. 313. Thereafter, Christian shrines and monuments appeared throughout the territory held by the Eastern Roman, or Byzantine, Empire. Thus, both Jews and Christians came to see Palestine as the Holy Land, the birthplace of their respective faiths.

Meanwhile, the Nabataeans thrived under Roman rule, exploiting important trade roads guarded by forts that had been set up at strategic distances. Operating from a secure base close to the caravan routes that stretched from Syria to the Arabian Peninsula, the Nabataeans grew prosperous in the fifth century, but changes in the routes of the caravans gradually halted their income. By the seventh century, Petra was a dead city, its location known only to Bedouin traders (a nomadic Arab people).

The Muslim Conquest

During this time, Arabs from the south also entered the struggle for power within Palestine. Although they had always represented potential strength, the scattered peoples of the Arabian Peninsula (which includes Saudi Arabia, Yemen, Oman, Qatar, and other countries) had lived, fought, and worshiped in small, disunited groups. In the early seventh century, they were united in the new faith of Islam, which called for submission to the will of God as taught by the prophet Muhammad. Islam's holy book is called the Quran.

After Muhammad's death in 632, his teachings inspired his followers (called Muslims) to spread their faith throughout the region. Within twenty years of the prophet's death, Muslim Arabs had spread Islam far to the north and east from the Arabian Peninsula—including to modern-day Jordan—as well as westward into North Africa. Like the Jews and Christians before them, the followers of Islam constructed places of worship in the Holy Land of Palestine.

Islam provided the push toward a centralized political power. Taxes were collected and redistributed for the common good. Islam attempted to bring the individual, the local community, and the entire society under a single religious authority. Descendants of Muhammad automatically held positions of power. They formed a ruling class and were called imams.

The Umayyad Dynasty and the Crusaders

During and after the period of the Muslim conquest, leadership of the Muslim kingdom passed to a line of caliphs, or successors. When the fourth caliph, Muhammad's son-in-law Ali, was assassinated, Mu'awiyah ascended to the caliphate. Thus began the Umayyad dynasty (661–750), or family of rulers. The Umayyads had their capital first in the middle of Mesopotamia (modern-day Iraq) and then in Damascus, Syria. The dynasty ruled the region according to Sharia, or Muslim law. Provincial governors oversaw local populations and were responsible to the caliph. Muslim civil law applied only to Muslims, while separate religious communities of Jews and Christians were bound by their own codes.

Later caliphs, however, did not strictly follow the teachings of the prophet Muhammad. Although Muhammad had stressed the dignity and virtue of nomadic life, the later Umayyad caliphs developed a pampered lifestyle. Jordan, close to Damascus and the desert, became a favorite resort where traditional Arab tents were replaced by castles and elegant, costly, dome-shaped structures. In 750 the Abbasids, a rival group, conquered the Umayyads and moved the capital to Baghdad, Iraq.

Muslim dominance in the region faced a challenge late in the eleventh century, when a new, completely foreign force came to the area—the Frankish, or western European, crusaders. In 1095 Pope Urban II, leader of the Roman Catholic Church, responded to European fears of Muslim expansion by calling for a crusade to capture and bring the Holy Land—Palestine—under Christian rule. Thousands of European soldiers invaded the region, and Jordan and Palestine fell under European control. The crusaders built churches and Christian shrines to express their faith and castles to control the caravan routes throughout the region.

Muslims and crusaders continued to fight over the Holy Land for most of the next century. Ultimately, Saladin, a Sunni scholar and soldier, led the Arab armies to

a clear victory on the western shore of the Sea of Galilee, effectively bringing the Crusades to an end.

Turkish Domination and the Rise of Arab Nationalism

In the meantime, invaders from central Asia had conquered much of southwestern Asia. One group, the Ottoman Turks, had occupied Anatolia (mainland Turkey) and parts of Persia. By 1516 they had annexed Syria, Jordan, and Palestine. The Ottoman Turks, who had adopted Islam earlier, reigned as strict overlords in the region for four hundred years, and social and economic development suffered from Ottoman neglect.

The Ottomans adopted a style of military government that required the least effort for the most profit. Although order was firmly enforced in the cities, areas outside the city were allowed to fall into lawlessness, and outlaws constantly harassed farmers who lived beyond the protective boundaries. The Turks did not bother the raiders of the Bedouin, as long as taxes were paid. The system of allowing limited self-rule to different religious groups continued. This policy was known as the millet system.

The Ottomans did introduce the Hejaz Railway, which reached the country in 1908. Trains ran from Istanbul, Turkey, to Aleppo in Syria, over to Damascus, down to Amman, and eventually to the end of the line in Medina in Saudi Arabia. In general, however, Ottoman rule hampered the political, economic, and technological development of the Arab world, a handicap that has persisted into modern times.

The Hejaz Railway still operates between Damascus, Syria, and Amman, Jordan. Several of the historical routes have never been rebuilt after British and Arab forces blew them up during the Great Arab Revolt (1917–1918).

By the end of the nineteenth century, internal and external forces were weakening the Ottoman Empire. Nationalism—the idea of promotion of one's home state or nation above other concerns—was gaining ground, as the empire's many states began to resist foreign rule. Meanwhile, European powers—in particular the British, French, and Russians—sought to gain power in the region and posed a threat due to their superior military power.

Yet at this time, the empire's Arab peoples lacked the unity to muster a challenge to Ottoman rule. But other events set the stage for an Arab revolt in the first decades of the twentieth century. In 1909 a Turkish group called the Committee of Union and Progress deposed the Ottoman sultan Abdulhamid II. This nationalist group, later known as the Young Turks, opposed government tolerance of millets. The Young Turks wanted to absorb other cultures into that of the Turks. Many Arabs resisted this goal, and so the policies of the Young Turks helped to forge a more unified Arab resistance.

Arab nationalists in Lebanon and Syria began to work toward Arab freedom within the Ottoman Empire. They founded secret societies, which published underground (secret) pamphlets and posters calling for an end to foreign control of Palestine and the Arabian Peninsula.

At the same time, the remote desert groups of Jordan and Arabia engaged in efforts to disrupt Ottoman trade. Although these groups had no unified political voice, they helped to weaken the economic base of the empire.

Arab unity made another step forward in 1914 when Hussein ibn Ali—the grand emir (prince) of Mecca and a sharif, or direct descendant of Muhammad—came forward to serve as a link between Arabs of the cities and the desert societies. After negotiating with Arabs in Syria and Lebanon through various secret organizations, Sharif Hussein of the Hashemite family was accepted as the spokesperson for a large percentage of the Arab peoples.

⊙ Conflicting Agreements

That same year, World War I (1914–1918) began in Europe. This conflict pitted the French, British, Russians, and their allies against Germany, the Austro-Hungarian Empire, and their allies. Hoping to reduce or remove British, French, and Russian influence from the Middle East, the Ottoman Empire chose to fight on the side of the Germans and Austro-Hungarians.

Thus the British and the Arabs had a mutual interest in defeating the Ottomans. But the two parties had conflicting goals. While the Arabs sought independence, the British sought a stronger presence in the region.

Sharif Hussein *(center, front)* was the last of the Hashemite monarchs to rule over Medina, Mecca, and the Hejaz (a region in western Saudi Arabia) in an unbroken line from 1201 to 1925.

Nevertheless, in exchange for Arab agreement to fight the Turks openly, Britain's high commissioner Sir Henry MacMahon promised Sharif Hussein territory for Arab independence under a "Sharifian Arab government." A number of letters exchanged by MacMahon and Hussein—called the MacMahon Letters—set up rough boundaries for this area, which included modern-day Jordan, Syria, Iraq, Lebanon, and the Arabian Peninsula.

Meanwhile, the British had made other agreements that would eventually conflict with their promises of true Arab independence. The British signed a secret agreement with the French and Russians. The Sykes-Picot Agreement laid out plans for the Middle East to be divided into French and British zones of control, with modern-day Jordan falling under British rule. Palestine would be jointly controlled by France, Britain, and Russia. For the time being, the Sykes-Picot Agreement was kept a secret.

On June 5, 1916, Hussein launched the Arab Revolt against Ottoman rule. His sons, Abdullah and Faisal, along with other prominent sheikhs (chiefs), led desert forces from Jordan and Arabia. With money, arms, and British technical advisers (the most famous of whom was T. E. Lawrence, or Lawrence of Arabia), Hussein succeeded in stopping traffic along the Hejaz Railway. In October he proclaimed himself king of the Arabs.

The following year, the British also made promises to the Zionist (Jewish) immigrants located in Palestine. (A movement called Zionism had begun in the late nineteenth century to establish a Jewish homeland. Theodor Herzl had formed the World Zionist Organization and called for

Jews to immigrate to Palestine, site of the ancient kingdom of Israel.) The British saw the Jews as a potential ally in the region.

Discussions took place in November 1917 between the British foreign secretary Arthur James Balfour and the leaders of the Zionists. Together they produced a document known as the Balfour Declaration, which promised British assistance in the creation of a home for Jews in Palestine. The Balfour Declaration aroused anger from Arabs, despite British assurances that non-Jewish peoples in Palestine would not be subject to Jewish rule.

But that same month, the new Russian government made the Sykes-Picot Agreement public. And so it was exposed that the British had made three different and conflicting agreements about the future makeup of the Middle East. Yet Britain again reassured Arab leaders. The war effort ended in 1918, when British forces defeated the Turks at Megiddo (in modern-day Israel) in September and when troops led by Hussein's son Faisal, took Damascus, Syria, in early October. The peace agreement with Turkey was signed on October 31, 1918.

> "His Majesty's government view with favour the establishment in Palestine of a national home for the Jewish people and will use their best endeavours to facilitate the achievement of this object, it being clearly understood that nothing shall be done which may prejudice the civil and religious rights of existing non-Jewish communities in Palestine."
>
> —The Balfour Declaration, November 1917

Emir Faisal established an independent Arab government at Damascus in October 1918. But the Arabs' goal of true independence would not be achieved. At the international conference held in San Remo, Italy, in 1920, France and Great Britain divided Syria, Palestine, and what would become Transjordan between themselves. French troops forced Faisal to leave Syria in July 1920.

Transjordan

Meanwhile, Winston Churchill, who was the British secretary for the colonies at the time, reserved a portion of Palestine for Arab rule, although the British were to remain in military and supervisory roles. Thus the East Bank of the Jordan River became known as Transjordan (beyond the Jordan), while the West Bank became a British administrative colony. Because a majority of the desert societies supported Hussein's Hashemite family, the British named Hussein's son Abdullah ruler of Transjordan in

1921. Transjordanian independence was declared on May 15, 1923, although the British remained effectively in control.

The British supplied development funds and helped Abdullah raise and train a national fighting force called the Arab Legion. This unit consisted of Arab soldiers but was commanded by British officers. Through a series of treaties, Transjordan moved closer to complete independence. The West Bank, on the other hand, remained under full British control. It had become a place of great tension by the mid-1930s. As restrictions against Jews spread in Germany, thousands of Jews immigrated to Palestine. Arabs on both sides of the river were alarmed at the increase in the Jewish population, which they saw as a threat to their own control of the region.

Jewish emigration to Palestine accelerated during World War II (1939–1945). In that conflict, German forces seized control of much of Europe and imposed German leader Adolf Hitler's "Final Solution," which called for the annihilation of the Jewish race. The German actions, known as the Holocaust, involved the murder of about 6 million Jews. Following the discovery of these atrocities near the end of the war, the urgency to allow the Jews their own homeland in Palestine grew.

HOPE FOR PEACE BETWEEN JEWS AND ARABS

In 1920 Prince Faisal, brother of King Abdullah of Transjordan and future king of Iraq, sent a letter to an American Zionist, Felix Frankfurter, expressing his hopes that Jews and Arabs could live in peace together in Palestine:

"We feel the Arabs and Jews are cousins in race, having suffered similar op-pressions at the hands of powers stronger than them-selves, and by a happy coin-cidence have been able to take the first step toward the attainment of their national goals together. We Arabs, especially the educated among us, look with the deepest sympathy on the Zionist movement. . . . We will wish the Jews a most hearty welcome home."

The Arab-Israeli Conflict

The influx of Jews to Palestine led to increased tensions between Arabs and Jews, and in 1947 the British government asked the United Nations (UN) to help solve the problem. According to the plan devised by the UN, Palestine was divided into two states—Arab and Jewish. Jerusalem—home to many Muslim, Christian, and Jewish holy sites—was to be put under international control. The British withdrew from Palestine, and on May 14, 1948, the Jews proclaimed the independent State of Israel. Immediately thereafter, several Arab nations, including

Egypt, Syria, Transjordan, Lebanon, Iraq, and Saudi Arabia attacked the Jewish state.

Transjordan's Arab Legion took the West Bank and captured the Old City of Jerusalem, which contained many ancient Muslim holy sites. But Israel defeated the combined Arab forces and gained strategic territory along its borders. The following year, Abdullah declared himself king of Jordan and ordered that the country's name be changed to the Hashemite Kingdom of Jordan.

Meanwhile, hundreds of thousands of Palestinian Arabs had fled Palestine, with the majority of them seeking refuge in Jordan. The UN set up several camps for these people to live in. The Palestinian refugees soon outnumbered the native Jordanian population by two to one. Jobs were scarce for the newcomers, most of whom lived in poverty in the camps. Many blamed the king for their problems.

The new population began to push for a limit to the power of the king and the cabinet. In April 1950, elections for a representative body were held in both the West Bank and East Bank of Jordan, but Abdullah remained effectively in control of the country. The king had the power to dissolve (dismiss) the legislature, to appoint and remove high-ranking government officials, and to create and impose laws.

Shortly after the elections, the Jordanian legislature formally authorized the annexation (taking over) of the West Bank. The move was criticized by many Arabs, who felt that King Abdullah was acting in his own interests, not in the interests of the Palestinians. Abdullah's attitude toward Israel further angered the Palestinians, as well as other Arabs. While other Arab leaders refused to recognize or

ABDULLAH AND ISRAEL

Unlike other Arab leaders, King Abdullah quickly accepted the reality of a Jewish state in Palestine. He realized the Arabs lacked the unity and military strength to destroy Israel. Although his Arab Legion did participate in the 1948 Arab-Israeli Conflict, this had been done to gain more territory—specifically, the West Bank—as opposed to destroying the new Jewish state. Shortly before his death, King Abdullah explained his views to an Israeli official:

"I want peace not because I have become a Zionist or care for Israel's welfare, but because it is in the interests of my people. I am convinced that if we do not make peace with you, there will be another war, and another war, and another war, and we would lose. Hence it is in the supreme interest of the Arab nation to make peace with you."

negotiate a peace agreement with the Jewish state, Abdullah showed a willingness to compromise with the Israelis. In 1950 Palestinians were angered by news that King Abdullah had negotiated with Israel. A year later, Abdullah was assassinated by a Palestinian.

The crown passed to Abdullah's second son, Talal, who resigned shortly thereafter because of mental illness. Talal's teenage son, Hussein ibn Talal, was declared King Hussein I on August 11, 1952. He assumed his duties in 1953 after reaching eighteen years of age.

Threats to Hussein's Reign

The young monarch inherited a kingdom in crisis. Arab leaders as well as Jordanian citizens criticized Hussein for his ties to Britain. (The new king had been educated in Britain, the Arab League was still commanded by British officers, and the Jordanian government relied on British financial aid.) They saw the new king as a threat to Arab nationalism.

King Hussein I

His Arab neighbors also armed Palestinian fighters, who then used Jordan as a base for attacks on Israel. The Israelis responded to these raids by attacking and destroying Jordanian villages.

At the same time, many Palestinians living in Jordan blamed the new king for their troubles. In December 1955, mass demonstrations broke out in Amman. The Egyptian government—seeking a more anti-Israeli and anti-British leadership in Jordan—encouraged these threats to Hussein's authority. Egyptian radio broadcasts, which could be heard in Jordan, accused Hussein of being a British "puppet."

To ease tensions within his country and with his neighbors, Hussein expelled Lieutenant General Sir John Bagot Glubb, the British commander of the Arab Legion. The move meant eventual loss of British funds, but it strengthened Hussein's bond with other Arab leaders. Saudi Arabia, Egypt, and Syria soon pledged to provide Jordan with financial aid (although Egypt and Syria did not keep their pledges). In addition, the U.S. government also began to provide Jordan with financial aid.

Dependence on foreign money left King Hussein in a difficult position. His ability to rule was curbed by his dependence on outside powers. Meanwhile, radical Arab nationalists, who called for a Palestinian revolt and for revenge against Israel, increased opposition to Hussein's reign throughout the next decade. But the king retained control through the loyal Jordanian Arab Army (formerly the Arab Legion) and by working aggressively to disrupt any organized threats to his rule.

Continuing Conflicts

In 1964 the Palestinians began to unite under a new force—the Palestine Liberation Organization (PLO)—whose purpose was to destroy Israel and to work for the return of Palestine to the Palestinians. The Palestine National Charter, drawn up by Palestinians at a conference in 1964, forbade the PLO to interfere in the internal affairs of any Arab country. Almost immediately, however, trouble developed in Jordan.

The PLO moved freely within the heavily populated Palestinian refugee camps, attempting to tax Palestinians, to train soldiers, and to distribute arms. When the Palestinian guerrilla organization Fatah was added to the PLO in 1964, the combined forces began to launch strikes against Israel from within Jordan. As in the previous decade, Israel used a policy of massive retaliation—destroying Arab settlements along the Jordanian border. In response to Israeli threats, Hussein signed a military alliance with Egypt on May 30, 1967.

In the Six-Day War that followed in June 1967, Israel quickly defeated Egypt, Jordan, and Syria while seizing the West Bank and all of Jerusalem from Jordan. Thus Jordan lost about one-third of its best agricultural land and its major tourist centers. About 200,000 additional Palestinian refugees fled to the East Bank. Soon after the war, Hussein postponed national elections for the House of Representatives, stating that they could not go forward while the Israelis were occupying a large portion of Jordanian territory (the West Bank). To stifle any unified opposition to his rule, the king also banned all political parties.

Israel's swift victory in the Six-Day War was a tremendous embarrassment for Jordan and its allies. Once again, Israel had proven its overwhelming military superiority. As a result, King Hussein began to engage in secret meetings with the Israelis, in hopes of negotiating a favorable peace plan that included the return of the West Bank. But no agreements were reached.

Meanwhile, the thousands of uprooted Palestinian peoples refused to accept the loss of their land. Following the Six-Day War, guerrilla groups connected to the PLO increased in size and strength. In October 1968, thousands of these

RESOLUTION 242

Following the Six-Day War of June 1967, the United Nations passed a resolution that tried to sort out the ongoing Arab-Israeli conflict. Resolution 242 called for Israeli forces to leave the West Bank and other areas it had taken over during the Six-Day War. Israel's Arab neighbors were called on to stop threatening Israel and to recognize the Jewish state's right to exist. None of the countries involved have ever carried out all of the actions called for in the resolution.

fighters—who called themselves fedayeen (those who sacrifice themselves)—marched through Amman in a show of strength and as a challenge to the Jordanian government. A month later, the fedayeen briefly invaded the U.S. embassy in Amman.

At first, King Hussein avoided any drastic action against the guerrilla groups. Their open defiance of Israel had made the fedayeen heroes in the Arab world, and he did not want to anger the general population by attacking them. But over time, the fedayeen's actions—which included attacks against Israel, airliner hijackings, and an assassination attempt against the king—forced Hussein to act.

By August 1970, fighting had broken out between the guerrillas and the Jordanian Arab Army. In violence that continued through most of September 1970, the PLO and other groups were defeated and driven from the capital of Amman and from most of the country. Opposition from guerrilla groups continued over the next year until Jordanian forces captured the last of the PLO bases.

Many of the guerrillas were pursued into Lebanon, where they tried to continue their operations. A radical wing, led by PLO chairman Yasser Arafat, named itself Black September in recognition of Palestinians killed in the September 1970 fighting. Over the next two years, Black September was responsible for several hijackings, the assassination of Jordanian prime minister Wafsi al-Tall in Cairo, Egypt, and the kidnapping and murder of Israeli athletes at the 1972 Olympic Games in Munich, West Germany.

Dispute over the West Bank

Jordan's economy continued to grow in the 1970s as funds from Kuwait, Saudi Arabia, and the United States reduced debts caused by Palestinian refugees and the war effort. The situation was further eased by the establishment of an "open bridges" policy between Israeli West Bank and Jordanian East Bank communities. Many Palestinians returned to the West Bank when it became safe to do so.

Meanwhile, King Hussein continued to work toward solving the problem of a homeland for the Palestinians. In the early 1970s, Hussein proposed a federation plan to join the East and West Banks under the name United Arab Kingdom, with a national capital at Amman. The reaction of the Arab world was hostile. The move was seen as an attempt by Hussein to take control of land that rightfully belonged to independent Palestinians. In 1974 at the Arab Summit Conference in Rabat, Morocco, the PLO—not Jordan, as Hussein had hoped—was named the official representative group for the Palestinians.

The conclusions of the Rabat conference would make peace between Israel and its neighbors next to impossible, however. Both

A woman casts her vote during the 2003 parliamentary elections in Amman, Jordan. Jordanian women earned the right to vote in 1974. However, they did not have the chance to exercise this right until 1984, when the first elections in seventeen years took place.

Israel and the United States—which held great influence in the region through its economic and military strength—considered the PLO a terrorist organization and refused to negotiate with it. Nevertheless, Hussein officially stood by the decisions reached at Rabat. He supported several peace proposals, always maintaining that the PLO must be involved as representatives of the Palestinian people.

As the 1970s drew to a close, Jordan and the rest of the Middle East began to struggle with economic problems. In the early 1980s, the price of oil began to drop, causing an economic recession throughout the region. The economic hardship that followed led to increasing unrest among the Jordanian population. To ease these tensions, Hussein began to allow citizens more participation in the political process. These changes resulted in elections for the House of Representatives in 1984—the first in seventeen years and the first in which women were allowed to vote.

Hussein also embraced measures aimed at strengthening Jordan's claim as caretaker of the West Bank. Even after the Six-Day War, the Jordanian government had paid the salaries of teachers and other government workers in the Israeli-occupied West Bank. In 1986 he revealed a plan to invest $1.3 billion to reconstruct the West Bank and the disputed Gaza Strip, a tiny piece of land along the Mediterranean between Israel and Egypt.

But ongoing attempts at reaching a peace settlement between the Israelis and Arabs continued to fail, and Israeli troops continued to occupy the West Bank. In late 1987, a Palestinian intifada (uprising) broke out in the Israeli-occupied territories. Palestinian civilians showed their anger against Israel and Jordan with mass demonstrations and mob violence. King Hussein announced in the next year that

Jordan was giving up its official claim to the West Bank. The move meant that the Palestinians living in the region would lose Jordanian development funds and government jobs.

Jordan suffered another economic downturn after Iraq invaded Kuwait in the summer of 1990. King Hussein—whose government had come to rely on Iraqi financial aid—refused to condemn Iraq's invasion, despite the fact that nearly all of his Arab neighbors had done so. (Jordanian public opinion strongly supported Iraqi president Saddam Hussein's actions.) Thus Jordan lost much of its trade, oil supply, and foreign aid. Its relations with its Arab neighbors and the United States were seriously damaged.

Steps toward Peace

After Iraq's defeat in early 1991, negotiations began between Israel, Palestinian representatives, and several Arab states, including Jordan. The result was the 1993 Oslo Agreements—named after the capital of Norway, where most of the negotiations took place—which allowed for the election of an interim (temporary) Palestinian government in parts of the West Bank and Gaza Strip, as well as further negotiations between Israel and the PLO.

The Oslo Agreements were hailed as a huge step toward peace between the Palestinians and Israel. Jordan responded to these promising developments by signing its own peace agreement with Israel in October 1994. The plan included Israeli-Jordanian cooperation in trade, sharing electricity, and fighting crime. The U.S. government rewarded Jordan with generous financial and military aid.

At first, peace with Israel created many positive results for the Jordanian economy. Tourism, trade, and foreign investment increased dramatically, as people and businesses sought to take advantage of Jordan's improved security and stability. Yet millions of Palestinian refugees remained in Jordan. For these people, the future remained uncertain.

But the good feelings between Jordan and Israel did not last long. In May 1996, Israeli elections brought to power a government hostile to the peace process. At the same time, the Palestinian Authority—the new Palestinian interim government—failed to stop Palestinians from engaging in violence against Israelis. The peace process quickly began to crumble, but King Hussein would not live to see it fall apart completely.

Visit www.vgsbooks.com to find links to more information about Jordan's history and government, including links to UN Security Council Resolution 242 and the Jordan-Israel Peace Treaty document.

◉ A New Monarch

In February 1999, King Hussein died after a long battle with cancer. His son Abdullah succeeded him, ascending the throne as King Abdullah II. Like his father about forty-six years before him, the thirty-seven-year-old new king faced a host of challenges.

In October 2000, Palestinians launched a new intifada against Israel. Palestinian militants began sending suicide bombers into Israeli territory. These attackers usually blew themselves up in buses, restaurants, and other crowded locations to cause maximum death and injury to Israeli civilians. The Israeli military responded with massive military raids against Palestinians in the West Bank and Gaza. This circle of suicide bombings and massive retaliation continues.

Violence and turmoil have also threatened Jordan from the east, in Iraq. King Abdullah II joined his Arab neighbors in condemning the 2003 U.S.-led invasion of Iraq to oust Iraqi leader Saddam Hussein. In light of their country's past as a possession of the British, many Jordanians were deeply hostile toward the idea of Western armies invading Arab lands. After the U.S.-led forces quickly toppled Saddam Hussein's government in April, some Jordanians crossed the Iraqi border to engage in terrorist attacks against U.S. forces and others helping with Iraq's reconstruction. A number of these people have connections to the international terrorist group al-Qaeda, which is blamed for the September 11, 2001, attacks on the United States.

One of the most prominent terrorist leaders in Iraq is a Jordanian known as Abu Musab al-Zarqawi. Zarqawi is believed to be responsible for numerous attacks against U.S. forces and has been blamed for the kidnapping and murder of several persons who were cooperating with the Iraqi rebuilding effort.

In 2004 the situation in post-invasion Iraq remained a major concern for Jordanians. Some fear that Iraq will erupt into civil war, leading to a new influx of refugees to Jordan or the emergence of a government that might be hostile to Jordan. Many Jordanians fear that the instability in Iraq could destabilize Jordan's government. In mid-2004, Abdullah II attempted to ease the situation by offering to send Jordanian troops to Iraq. The new Iraqi government thanked the king for the offer but did not immediately accept it.

◉ Government

In accordance with the Constitution of 1952, Jordan is headed by a male hereditary monarch, who has power over the executive, legislative, and judicial branches of the government. The monarch appoints a council of ministers—which is led by a prime minister—to assist with executive duties. The monarch also signs and executes all laws,

Islamist activist Hayat al-Massimi *(center, left)* was the only Muslim woman to win a seat in Jordan's 2003 parliamentary elections.

declares war, concludes peace, commands the armed forces, and approves amendments to the constitution.

The bicameral (two-house) Parliament forms the legislative branch. The members of the House of Representatives are elected to four-year terms by citizens eighteen years of age or older. Women voted for the first time in 1984. The monarch appoints the members of the senate, whose delegates hold office for eight-year terms. The monarch holds the right to dissolve Parliament at any time. Most Parliament seats are reserved for Muslims. The Jordanian judicial system consists of three kinds of courts. The first type is made up of civil courts. Magistrates' courts, the lowest in the civil system, hear minor criminal and civil cases. More important cases being tried for the first time go to courts of first instance. At the top of the ladder is the Supreme Court, which presides over cases against the state, hears appeals, and interprets the law.

The second category is made up of religious courts for both Muslims and non-Muslims. These courts rule on personal matters, such as marriage and divorce. The third category consists of special courts, such as land, government, property, municipal, custom, and tax courts. All judges for the judiciary are appointed and are sometimes dismissed by the monarch.

Jordan is divided into five administrative units called governorates. A governor appointed by the monarch heads each district. Governors have sole authority for all government departments and development projects in their respective areas. In the cities, mayors and their elected councils take care of local affairs.

THE PEOPLE

Jordan's population is estimated to be 5.6 million. Like its Middle Eastern neighbors, the country experienced a population explosion in the second half of the twentieth century. Before the formation of Transjordan in 1921, the number of people living in the area was just 230,000. By 1938 the population of Transjordan had grown to 300,000. Many of these were Palestinians who had fled their homes to escape the increasing violence between Arabs and Jews in Palestine.

By 1952, four years after the 1948 Arab-Israeli Conflict, Jordan's population had grown to 680,000, with nearly half being Palestinian refugees. Twenty-seven years later, in 1979, the number of people living in Jordan had more than tripled, reaching 2.1 million. In recent decades, Jordan's population has continued to swell, reaching 3.2 million in 1990 and 5.6 million in 2004.

This rapid increase has placed a strain on the Jordanian government's ability to provide services to its citizens. In particular, Jordan's large population and dry desert climate have made water shortages a

way of life. But despite these challenges, Jordanians have consistently increased their standard of living over the decades through improvements in housing, education, and health care. As a result, the Jordanian government provides its people with some of the best health care and education systems in the Middle East.

Ethnic Mixture

Jordan's population is the most homogeneous (composed of one group) in the Middle East. Nearly all Jordanians—98 percent—are Arabs. The term Arab was originally associated with the camel-herding nomadic tribes of the Arabian Peninsula. In more recent centuries, it has been used to describe settled people whose native language is Arabic, no matter what country they live in. In addition to sharing a common tongue, nearly all Arabs also follow the same religion—Islam. Arabs are the majority population in most Middle Eastern countries.

Many **modern Jordanians** enjoy the same sports and liesure activities common in the West. These four women are members of the Middle East's first female boxing team.

Jordan's Arab population consists of two groups—Palestinians and Bedouin. Most Palestinians in Jordan are refugees or descendants of refugees from the old territory of Palestine, although they enjoy full Jordanian citizenship. The exact number of Palestinians in Jordan is not known. The Jordanian government states that 43 percent of Jordanians are Palestinian, but most other estimates place the number much higher— perhaps as high as half or even 60 percent. About two-thirds of Jordan's Palestinians live within or near the ten UN refugee camps in Jordan, or within three "unofficial" (not UN-run) camps that are located in the cities of Amman, Zarqa, and Madaba.

The Palestinian refugee camps are crowded and bustling. The UN and the Jordanian government provide schooling and free medical care to the inhabitants. While many Palestinian refugees hope to return to their old homes west of the Jordan River, others have abandoned this goal. Most of the Palestinians who no longer live in the refugee camps have moved into Jordan's cities, towns, and villages. Many have become completely integrated into Jordanian society. Some have opened successful businesses or even entered into Jordanian politics.

While Palestinians and Bedouin generally live together peacefully, some tensions do exist. Because many Bedouin consider Palestinians to be only guests in their country, they look forward to the day when their neighbors can return to Palestine.

Visit www.vgsbooks.com to find links with information about Bedouins and other groups in Jordan. You can also find links to learn more about the Palestinian refugee camps in Jordan.

The Bedouin are the original inhabitants of Jordan and make up the majority of the non-Palestinian population. This ethnic group is famous for its traditional lifestyle. Since ancient times, Bedouin have roamed the deserts of the Middle East, moving from place to place in search of water and pastureland for their camels, sheep, and goats. In modern times, only a small percentage of Bedouin continue to live this traditional way of life. Many Jordanian Bedouin have settled on farms or moved to cities to find work.

Jordan's non-Palestinian Arabs are sometimes referred to as East Bankers. Most have Bedouin roots, and the Bedouin traditions of courtesy, courage, and hospitality run strong in Jordanian culture. The ruling Hashemite family has Bedouin roots, and Bedouins make up a large percentage of the Jordanian armed forces. Throughout his rule, King Hussein often turned to his traditional allies for support during turbulent periods.

Jordan's small—2 percent or less—non-Arab population consists mostly of Circassians and Chechens. These people are the descendants of Muslims who were driven from their homes in Circassia and Chechnya (in southwestern Russia) by Russian authorities in the late 1800s. They live mostly in Amman and Zarqa and total about 35,000 people.

Language

Arabic is the official language of Jordan. Virtually all Jordanians speak Arabic, a Semitic language that originated on the Arabian Peninsula and that is related to Hebrew and other ancient tongues of the Middle East. The Arabic alphabet has twenty-eight characters and is read from right to left and from the top to the bottom of a page. Nearly 200 million people worldwide speak Arabic.

Spoken Arabic is quite different from written Arabic. Written, or classical, Arabic is the language of the Quran, the holy book of Islam. It is used in newspapers, books, and other writings and is virtually the same throughout the Arab world. Spoken, or colloquial, Arabic has many different dialects, which differ in their use of vocabulary, pronunciation, grammar, and sentence structure. In many cases, the differences between dialects are such that a speaker of one dialect cannot understand most

"Insha Allah" is an Arabic phrase often heard in Arab countries. It means, "if God wills it," and reflects Muslims' surrender to the power and will of God. (Islam means "surrender.") The phrase is used when making a hopeful prediction—"I will feel better tomorrow, insha Allah,"—or in answer to a question: "Will I see you later? Insha Allah."

other dialects. In Jordan only two different dialects are spoken—one among urban Jordanians and another among rural citizens.

In addition to Arabic, many educated middle- and upper-class Jordanians also speak English. Nearly all Jordanians working in the tourist industry speak English, and most urban street signs in Jordan include English translations. Even less educated Jordanians know at least some English, and an English-speaking tourist would likely be able to get around the country without knowing much or any Arabic.

Education

When the nation of Transjordan was founded in the early 1920s, virtually no formal education system existed. In the decades since, Jordan's education system has grown to be one of the region's best. This success can be easily seen through the dramatic rise in literacy rates—the percentage of people over the age of fifteen who can read and write—over the last several decades. In 1961 the literacy rate in Jordan was only 32 percent. But this number has steadily increased in recent decades, from 74 percent in 1987 to 79 percent in the early 1990s. In the early 2000s, Jordan has a literacy rate of 91 percent—the second-highest in the region, after Israel. In comparison, many of Jordan's neighbors have significantly lower literacy rates, such as Iraq (40 percent) and Egypt (58 percent). Jordanian girls also enjoy more access to education than do girls living in other Arab countries. The literacy rate for women—86 percent—is the highest among women in the Arab world.

The Jordanian Ministry of Education provides public schooling to virtually all school-age children, including those living in sparsely populated areas. Every village or community with ten or more school-age children has access to public education, and more than 95 percent of Jordanian children go to school regularly.

Attendance is mandatory through the tenth grade. After com-

COMPARING THE NUMBERS

Jordan enjoys one of the highest literacy rates in the Middle East. Its numbers compare favorably to other nations of the world.

Selected Literacy Rates:

Percentage of People over the Age of Fifteen Who Can Read and Write

United States: 97
Canada: 97
Israel: 95
Mexico: 92
Jordan: 91
Lebanon: 87
Kuwait: 83
Saudi Arabia: 79
Syria: 77
Egypt: 58
Iraq: 40

Two schoolgirls work on an experiment in science class. Jordanian women have more access to **education** than do other Arab women.

pleting the tenth grade, many students move on to attend two years of secondary school. Jordan has two kinds of secondary schools—general schools that emphasize many different subjects and applied schools that specialize in vocational (skills or trades) courses. Some graduates of secondary schools then move on to higher education at one of Jordan's colleges or universities.

The Jordanian Ministry of Education has also placed a strong emphasis on higher education. Jordan has many community colleges, which provide education and training for such careers as teaching, social work, nursing, computer programming, and pharmacology. The country also has six public and twelve private universities. The largest and oldest of these is Jordan University in Amman, which was founded in 1962. Other universities in Jordan include Yarmuk University in Irbid and Mu'tah University in Karak. Although the Jordanian universities are relatively new, they are considered by some to be the best state-supported institutions of higher learning in the Arab Middle East, and they attract many students from other Arab countries.

Health

A study of some of Jordan's health statistics over the past several decades shows the country's rapid progress from a largely undeveloped country into one of the most progressive nations in the region. For example, in 1965, life expectancy in Jordan was 50 years. By 1986 this number had increased to 64 years. Life expectancy has continued to grow in Jordan since, reaching nearly 70 years in the early 2000s.

Part of the reason for the increase in life expectancy is the tremendous decrease in Jordan's infant mortality rate. Between 1981 and 1991, Jordan achieved the fastest annual rate of decline in infant mortality of any country—from 70 deaths per 1,000 live births to 37 deaths per 1,000 live births. Since then Jordan's infant mortality rate has continued to drop. The most recent statistics list 27 deaths per 1,000 live births. These numbers remain high, however, in comparison to some of Jordan's neighbors and more developed Western countries. (For example, the infant mortality rate in the United States is 7 deaths per 1,000 live births.)

Another factor in the jump in life expectancy has been the spread of sanitation (sewers, garbage disposal) and potable water services—services vital to curbing the spread of infectious disease. In 1950 only 10 percent of Jordan's population had access to sanitation and potable water. In the early 2000s, the percentage had increased to 99 percent.

The Jordanian government's commitment to childhood immunization programs has also helped to increase life expectancy in the country. In 1988 Jordan achieved universal childhood immunization, meaning nearly every Jordanian child had been vaccinated for common diseases such as measles, mumps, and polio. More recent statistics show that 98 percent of Jordanian children are fully immunized.

Like most Middle Eastern countries, Jordan has largely avoided the global HIV (human immunodeficiency virus) and AIDS (acquired immunodeficiency disorder) epidemic. Fewer than 0.1 percent of the population has HIV or the disease it causes, AIDS. Jordan's conservative Islamic culture—which strongly discourages both sexual promiscuity and drug use—is a key factor in this low rate of infection.

Jordan's national health care program provides the country's citizens with affordable health care. The program—combined with the country's modern hospitals and clinics and well-trained medical personnel—are the main reasons for the dramatic improvements to Jordan's health services in recent decades. For every 10,000 Jordanians, there are 28 doctors, 10 nurses, 7 dentists, 9 pharmacists, and 16 hospital beds. These totals make Jordan's health services among the best-equipped in the Middle East. But the quality of medical care is not the same throughout the country. While hospitals and clinics in urban areas such as Amman, Irbid, Zarqa, and Aqaba are modern and use up-to-date equipment, medical facilities in rural areas often lack adequate equipment and well-trained staff.

CULTURAL LIFE

Jordan's culture is centered on Islam—the country's official religion—and Arab traditions. Jordanians share many traditions with their Arab Muslim neighbors—such as a deep faith in God, strong loyalty to and respect for the family unit, and generous hospitality toward guests. Yet Jordanian society is more open than some of its more conservative neighbors.

This openness is most clearly displayed in the place of women in Jordanian society. For example, by law, women in Saudi Arabia—a very conservative country—must wear a traditional black abaya (dress) and veil in public. Few Jordanian women follow these restrictions, although they are expected to dress modestly. Jordanian women also have the freedom to hold a wider variety of jobs—some have even served in Jordan's legislature—than do women in neighboring countries. Women in Jordan also have access to a full education, including higher education, and have had the right to vote since 1974.

But Jordanian society remains conservative compared to Western standards. For example, parents often arrange Jordanian marriages—

although couples are rarely forced to marry against their wishes. And young Jordanian men and women are forbidden to spend any time together without the supervision of an adult.

▶ Religion

The vast majority of Jordanians are Muslims. About 92 percent of the population is made up of Sunni Muslims. This religious base is reflected in the country's Constitution of 1952, which states that the king and his successors must be Muslims, born of Muslim parents. (This restriction has been ignored for King Abdullah II, whose mother was a non-Muslim.) At the same time, freedom of religion is guaranteed in the Constitution, and Jordan has traditionally accepted worshipers of other faiths.

For most Jordanians, Islam is not just a religion, but a way of life. Islam revolves around the five *arkan*, or pillars, of faith. Each pillar is a duty that all Muslims must perform.

As part of their duties required by the **second pillar of Islam,** Muslims gather for Friday prayers at a mosque in Amman.

The first pillar is called *shahada*, or recitation of the creed: "there is no God but Allah and Muhammad is his prophet." *Salat* (daily prayer), the second pillar, is satisfied by turning toward Mecca and praying five times each day at dawn, noon, midafternoon, sunset, and nightfall. The third duty is called *zakat*, or almsgiving, which is support for those who are crippled or poor. *Sawn* (fasting), the fourth pillar, requires every Muslim to fast from sunrise to sunset each day during the holy month of Ramadan. The fifth and final pillar of Islam requires Muslims to make the hajj, a journey to the holy city of Mecca in Saudi Arabia, at least once in their lifetime if they are financially and physically able to do so. Every year, thousands of Jordanians make this pilgrimage, while many thousands more Muslims pass through Jordan on their way to the holy city.

Throughout its history, Islam has had a tradition of tolerance toward people of other faiths. This tradition goes back to the days of the millet system of the Umayyad dynasty and the Ottoman Empire, when Jews and Christians were allowed to govern themselves according to their own traditions. In the 2000s, about 6 percent of Jordan's population is Christian. Christians are mostly of the Eastern Orthodox sect, followed in number by Roman Catholics and Protestants. A small number of Druze—a secretive sect that branched off from Islam—live near the Syrian border, along with Samaritans and Circassians. The Samaritans are descendants of an ancient Jewish sect, and the Circassians are Sunni Muslims. Jordan's small Chechen population consists of mostly Shiite Muslims.

Literature, Music, and the Media

Muslims consider the Quran, the Muslim book of holy writings, as the perfect expression of the Arabic language. Its traditional, elegant writing style has greatly influenced literature in Arabic. But the Quran's influence on Jordanian (and virtually all Arab) writers goes beyond just literary style. For devout Muslims, content is very important, for Islam frowns upon works that are frivolous and harmful. On the other hand, writing that seeks to improve the world and glorify God is considered halal, or lawful and permitted.

As a relatively young country, Jordan is still developing its own distinctive national literature. At this point, no Jordanian writers have achieved significant fame beyond Jordan or the Arab world, and few Jordanian writers have seen their works translated into English.

Among Jordanians who have enjoyed acclaim with Arab readers, the most famous is the poet Mustafa Wahbi al-Tal (1899–1949). He is best known by his pen name, 'Arar. A lawyer and a judge, his works often focused on the idea of Arab nationalism. 'Arar's hometown of Irbid holds an annual poetry festival, and Jordan's most prestigious literary award is named after him.

Ibrahim Nasrallah (born 1954), a winner of the 'Arar Literary Award, is one of the Arab world's better-known poets. Like many writers who have lived and worked in Jordan, Nasrallah is a

"HONOR KILLINGS"

Conservative interpretations of Islam call on men to protect the honor of their family, sometimes in extreme ways. The most extreme result of these interpretations is the "honor killing," when a father or brother murders his daughter or sister for having brought shame to the family—for example, by engaging in premarital sex or adultery. Recent statistics show that about 25 percent of all solved murders in Jordan are "honor killings." Adding to the phenomenon is the fact that many Jordanian judges—as well as conservative Jordanians—are sympathetic to "honor killings" and believe such murders are proper under the circumstances. In the early 2000s, King Abdullah II, his brother, Prince Ali, and some members of the Jordanian government proposed legislation calling for stiffer penalties against such murders. But conservative members of Parliament protested against the legislation, and it was rejected.

Palestinian. Born in a Palestinian refugee camp in Jordan, he has written numerous poems about the plight of his people and has received many awards for his work.

Jordanian novels and short stories often feature urban settings but explore a wide variety of themes, from the political to the personal. Among prose writers, a handful of Jordanian women have made an impact. These include novelist and journalist Zahra Omer (1933–1999). A member of Jordan's small Circassian community, Omer's novel *Out of Sarouqah,* describes her ancestor's perilous flight from Russia at the end of the nineteenth century.

Jordanian readers also enjoy the works of writers from other Arab countries. Perhaps the most admired and widely read Arab author is an Egyptian—Naguib Mahfouz (born 1911), who won the Nobel Prize for Literature in 1988. Mahfouz is best known for his series of novels called the Cairo Trilogy, which follow the lives of a Cairene family through the first half of a twentieth century. He has also written dozens of novels and short stories, most of which have been translated into many languages.

Traditional Arabic music is highly improvisational and often is based on a five-tone—rather than the Western eight-tone—scale. Instrumentalists almost always accompany vocalists rather than performing purely instrumental music. Some of the most common classical instruments include the *oud,* a plucked instrument with nine to eleven strings; the *kemancha,* an Arabic violin made from a gourd, usually with only one string; and the *nay,* which resembles the flute.

Much of Jordan's modern popular music is lively and often features a star performer backed by an orchestra or a small band. Western instruments, such as violins and the piano, often play in harmony with Arabic instruments. Most Jordanians listen to music via radio broadcasts, as opposed to listening to CDs.

Jordan's media enjoys more freedom than the media in most Arab countries, but the Jordanian government does maintain some control over what is published in newspapers and broadcast on television and radio. On occasion, journalists have been arrested for being overly critical of the government, and politicians who do not share the government's views on policy have complained that the media rarely covers their concerns.

Far more Jordanians own radios than televisions. The country has approximately 560,000 televisions, compared to about 1.6 million radios. Radio Jordan has four stations, with two broadcasting in Arabic, and one each in English and French. Arabic programming includes Quran recitations, religious talk shows, news shows, and music. The English- and French-speaking stations broadcast mostly music and news.

To find out what's on TV in Jordan, visit www.vgsbooks.com. There you can also find links to numerous examples of Jordanian popular music.

The publicly operated Jordan Television has four channels. Channel One features news programs, talk shows, variety shows, and documentaries. Channel Two broadcasts coverage of a variety of national and international sporting events—including National Basketball Association games and World Wrestling Federation events from the United States. Channel Three is also known as the Jordan Movie Channel. During the day, the station shows cartoons and other children's programming. At night it shows movies in Arabic, English, and French. Channel Four is the Jordan Satellite Channel. Broadcasting throughout the Middle East via satellite, the channel features programming from Channel One as well as specially produced programs for international audiences. Many wealthy Jordanians own satellite dishes, which can pick up programming from around the world, including CNN and MTV. Israeli television broadcasts can also be viewed in southern Jordan.

Millions of Jordanians get their news from one of the country's five daily newspapers. Many magazines, both monthly and quarterly, are published by governmental and nongovernmental agencies.

Fewer than 500,000 Jordanians use the Internet on a regular basis, but this number is growing quickly due to the government's commitment to increasing computer literacy. Mobile phones are becoming increasingly popular in Jordan. Recent estimates show that more than 1.2 million citizens own mobile phones.

Handicrafts

Jordanian artisans employ techniques that blend methods as old as the Bronze Age and as new as power-driven drills. Reflecting the long influence of Islam—which discourages representations of the human body—designs used in carving, metalwork, and embroidery are mainly plant, flower, animal, and geometric motifs. Other designs, however, reflect Christian traditions, such as crosses and images of saints. Proverbs delicately engraved in Arabic and English are often part of the design.

Wood carving is a flourishing industry that caters to both tourists and local people. Most of the carvings are made from olive wood, and the finished objects are polished by hand with beeswax, varnish, or plastic coating.

Metalwork, such as costume jewelry and religious objects, may be made of silver, gold, or bronze. Goldsmiths work outside their shops and stalls at bazaars (street markets) using techniques handed down

Bedouin handicrafts are exhibited for sale in Jerash during the Jerash Festival of Culture and the Arts.

from generation to generation. Traditionally, mosaics adorn the walls and floors of both village dwellings and modern homes.

Most carpets for local trade are made of sheepskin and are used by Bedouin to cover the ground in their tents. Sheepskin rugs are washable, very strong, do not fade, and last for years. Villagers make rugs in bright wools from goat and camel threads that have been dyed in many colors.

Holidays and Festivals

Jordanians celebrate a wide variety of both religious and secular holidays. Muslim holidays follow the Islamic Hegira calendar, which is eleven days shorter than the Gregorian calendar used in the West. So each year, Islamic holidays fall eleven days earlier than on the previous year.

The holy month of Ramadan takes place on the ninth month of the Hegira calendar. During Ramadan, Muslims fast—do not eat or drink—from sunrise to sunset. Each day at sunset, extended families gather for a large meal—called *iftar*—followed by a special prayer service.

The end of Ramadan brings the three-day holiday known as Eid al-Fitr, during which Muslims dress up in new clothes, hold feasts, exchange presents, and visit the graves of relatives. Eid al-Fitr is one of two great Muslim festivals, the other being Eid al-Adha, which comes at the end of the annual hajj (the pilgrimage to Mecca occurs during the twelfth and final month of the Islamic calendar). Eid al-Adha celebrates the biblical story of the prophet Abraham, who was willing to sacrifice his son at God's command. At the last moment, God calls on Abraham to sacrifice a ram instead. In celebration of this legend, on Eid al-Adha, all Muslims who can afford to sacrifice an animal such as a goat, sheep, cow, or camel. Muslims also celebrate this holiday by exchanging gifts and visiting friends and family.

King Abdullah II *(left)* breaks his Ramadan fast at a mosque (house of prayer) in Amman.

Other Muslim holidays include the Islamic New Year, or Ras as-Sana; and Ashoura, the ninth and tenth days of the Islamic year; the prophet Muhammad's birthday, which falls during the third month of the Islamic calendar; and Eid al-Isra Wal Miraj. The latter is a feast, held on the twenty-seventh day of the seventh month, that celebrates Muhammad's nighttime visit to heaven from Jerusalem.

Jordan's Christians celebrate their religious holidays as well— Christmas and Easter, in particular. But Christian celebrations are much quieter than Muslim holidays, due to the smaller number of worshipers living in Jordan. But schools, government offices, and Christian businesses are closed for these occasions.

These same establishments are also closed on nonreligious holidays. These include New Year's Day (January 1); King Abdullah II's birthday (January 30); Arab League Day (March 22), in which Jordanians celebrate their Arab heritage; Labor Day (May 1), Independence Day (May 25); King Abdullah II's throne day (June 9), when Jordan's king officially assumed the throne. On Army Day and the Anniversary of the Great Arab Revolt (June 10), Jordanians honor their armed forces as well as the heroes who fought for Arab independence against the Ottoman Empire. King Hussein's birthday is celebrated on November 4.

Of course, Jordanians also mark major life events, such as births, weddings, and funerals. For example, in big cities and in villages, weddings call for dances and a festival that lasts for several days. Special songs accompany all such occasions. Jordanian farmers

JERASH FESTIVAL OF CULTURE AND THE ARTS

Every summer the city of Jerash hosts the Jerash Festival of Culture and the Arts. (Amman and other cities also hold related cultural events at the same time.) Singers, dancers, actors, and a variety of other performing artists from across Jordan and around the world come to perform. For a three-week period, festival audiences are entertained with musical performances, plays, movies, and dance performances.

observe the important moments in the agricultural calendar—plowing, planting, and harvesting—with festivals.

Many dances begin with the *debkah*—the pounding of feet on the floor to mark the rhythm. The dance known as the *sahjeh* is performed by Bedouin, and the Circassians have their own sword dance. The government has formed a national Circassian troupe that performs in local villages and on television and whose songs are played on the radio.

○ Food

Like all Arabs, Jordanians take pride in being generous hosts. This tradition of warm hospitality is best displayed at mealtimes, when a visitor can expect to be treated to whatever the host has to offer.

Jordanian cuisine is hearty and satisfying. In Aqaba charcoal-broiled and highly seasoned seafood—especially shrimp and lobster caught in the Red Sea—is popular. Jordanians enjoy *mansaf*, which is a Bedouin dish of lamb, yogurt, and rice.

MANSAF

Mansaf, the national dish of Jordan, is served for festive occasions of all sorts. In Jordan the yogurt sauce is usually made with dried goat-milk yogurt or whey that has been cooked with water, but plain yogurt will work as well. Jordanian mansaf is almost always made with lamb, but beef or chicken can also be used. (Chicken will only need to boil for about 30 minutes.) Vegetarian mansaf can be made with potatoes (boil 20 to 30 minutes) or tofu (bring to a boil and simmer 10 minutes).

1 lb. lean lamb, cut into bite-sized chunks

1 onion, chopped

¾ tsp. salt

¼ tsp. pepper

1 ½ c. medium or long-grain rice

¼ c. (½ stick) butter

3 c. hot water

1 tsp. salt

2 c. plain yogurt

4 to 6 pieces pita or other flat bread

1. Place lamb in a large saucepan or stockpot with onions and enough water to cover. Bring to a boil, add 3/4 tsp. salt and pepper, and cover. Boil 1 hour, or until meat is cooked all the way through.
2. When lamb has been cooking about 40 minutes, prepare rice. Rinse rice in water until water runs almost clear. In a saucepan or a wide, deep skillet, heat butter over medium heat until melted. Add rice, stirring well to coat grains with butter, and raise heat to high. Cook 3 to 4 minutes. Add hot water and 1 tsp. salt and bring to a boil. Reduce heat to medium, cover, and cook 15 to 20 minutes, or until all water has been absorbed. Turn off heat and leave rice covered to steam.
3. Remove lamb from heat and carefully scoop out about 1 c. of cooking water.
4. Place yogurt in a blender and blend on a low setting to make the yogurt runnier. If necessary, add a little bit of the reserved cooking water until the yogurt has the consistency of a creamy sauce.
5. Place yogurt in a second saucepan or pot and bring to a boil, stirring frequently. Try to always stir in the same direction. Reduce heat and leave to simmer for 10 to 15 minutes. Drain lamb and onions and add to yogurt sauce. Continue cooking 10 to 15 minutes more, or until sauce is thick.
6. Cover a large serving platter with flat bread in a single layer and pour a small amount of yogurt sauce over the bread. Pile the rice on top of the bread, pour lamb and yogurt over rice, and serve hot.

Serves 4 to 6 people.

Dinner in a Jordanian home usually begins with appetizers, such as small shish kebabs, roasted sardines, and tiny meatballs. The meal itself may start with a cup of spicy soup that combines lamb broth, onions, and green peppers. This first course may be followed by mansaf, hummus (a dip made from mashed chickpeas and pulped sesame seeds, usually served with bread), or roasted lamb. Beef is rarely eaten because cattle are too useful as work animals to slaughter them. The dessert may be chocolate pudding, a very sweet coconut dish, or a pastry, followed by fresh fruit and thick, dark Bedouin coffee.

Although there is a Muslim restriction against alcohol, some Jordanians enjoy beer, which is often served with olives and nuts at any time of the day. Jordanians delight in cold drinks. Small clay barrels hold homemade fruit concoctions, sold in stalls in every city and hamlet. These beverages are made from papayas, sugarcane, pineapples, oranges, and lemons.

NEIGHBORS IN SPORT

In 2004 Jordan lent a helping hand to its war-torn neighbor, Iraq, by assisting the Iraqi Olympic team in its bid to compete at the 2004 Olympic Games in Athens. The Jordanian government allowed the Iraqi Olympic men's soccer team to hold practices in Jordan and hosted the match that Iraq won to earn its spot at the games. In Athens, the Jordanian government paid for the Iraqi Olympic team's housing, training, and equipment costs. The Iraqi men's soccer team enjoyed an exciting run at the games, just missing out on an Olympic medal. The team provided the Iraqi people—and their Jordanian neighbors—with some good news amid the terror and violence of war.

◉ Sports and Recreation

Soccer is the most popular sport among Jordanians. Known as football in Jordan, it is the top spectator sport as well as the most popular sport to play for all ages. Teams from different cities and towns compete in league play, and the country comes to a virtual standstill during Jordan's national team matches. Love of soccer has even infected the royal family, and King Abdullah, like his father before him, is one of Jordan's number-one football fans.

The royal family also shares a love of auto racing with its citizens. King Hussein's love of fast cars was legendary. He owned several racing machines and was known to push them to the limit on the track (although he never raced in official competitions). Jordan's vast deserts are an excellent site for off-road rallies, and each spring the Royal Automobile Club of Jordan holds the Jordan International Rally, one of the

Camel racing is a unique sport enjoyed by Jordan's Bedouin community. Here two bedouins on camels prepare to compete against a 1933 Rolls Royce Phantom II in a 100-mile (160 km) race.

most popular races in the Middle East. (The future King Abdullah II competed in this race in the 1980s, finishing third in 1986 and 1988.) Meanwhile, Jordan's Bedouin enjoy watching and participating in a more traditional form of competition in the desert—camel races. Some camel racers have even made their sport into a profession.

Falconry (hunting with falcons) is another traditional sport that is enjoyed in Jordan. It is popular among the wealthy class, who can afford to purchase, raise, and train these beautiful hunting birds.

While participating in sports is a widespread activity among Jordanian youths, few adults engage in exercise and physical fitness. This attitude is common in the Arab world but is slowly changing as the health benefits of exercise are becoming more widely known. For young people, martial arts—such as tae kwon do and karate—are popular hobbies. Young Jordanians also enjoy volleyball and table tennis. In fact, the country rejoiced when fifteen-year-old table tennis player Zeina Shaaban became the first Jordanian to get past the opening round of an Olympic event at the 2004 Olympic Games in Athens.

Most Jordanian adults enjoy more leisurely activities, however. These include backgammon—a game that has been popular in the Middle East for centuries—and relaxing with friends and family at cafés.

A friendly game of backgammon

THE ECONOMY

Jordan shares many economic challenges with its Arab neighbors. The country has a very high unemployment rate—officially about 15 percent, but many estimates double this number. As much as 30 percent of the country lives in poverty, and Jordan's government is also burdened by a large budget deficit. A recent estimate lists Jordan's debt at U.S. $8 billion. This amount is about one-third of the country's entire gross domestic product (or GDP, the amount of goods and services produced in the country in a year) of U.S. $24 million. In addition, the ongoing political turmoil in the region requires Jordan to maintain a large—and expensive—military, which adds to its financial burden.

Yet, unlike most of its Arab neighbors, Jordan does not have an abundance of lucrative resources to exploit. Only a small amount of Jordan's land is suitable for farming. A lack of highly profitable mineral resources such as oil, combined with a large refugee population, has kept the country in a precarious economic situation.

Throughout its six decades as a fully independent nation, Jordan has always had to rely on foreign aid—first from Britain, then from its oil-rich neighbors and the United States—to remain afloat financially. Meanwhile, the country's economy has experienced several dramatic turns, all of them largely due to external events over which Jordan has had little control.

Jordan's official annexation of the West Bank in 1950 added a significant amount of fertile agricultural land to the country. For nearly two decades, the West Bank provided about one-third of the country's income, and Jordan's economy, boosted by foreign aid, grew steadily during this period.

But the 1967 Six-Day War brought this period of growth to an abrupt end. The loss of the West Bank to Israel was made worse by a new influx of Palestinian refugees, who strained the country's financial resources. Disruptive violence between Palestinians, Israelis, and Jordanians in the years following added to the country's struggles.

But by the early 1970s, Jordan's economy had experienced a dramatic upswing as all Arab countries profited from an unprecedented oil boom. During this time, Jordan indirectly benefited from the prosperity of its oil-rich neighbors through financial aid, trade, and via its position as a crossroads between the West, Africa, and Asia.

The Middle Eastern oil boom ended in the early 1980s, however, and Jordan's economic development slowed down. Yet the country's economy did better than its Arab neighbors during the decade. While the oil-rich states suffered through a recession, Jordan's economy was not as hard hit, partly because Jordan benefited from its economic ties to Iraq, which at the time was fighting a long and expensive war with Iran. These ties included access to Iraqi oil at low prices.

Financial links were part of the reason King Hussein supported Iraqi president Saddam Hussein after the Iraqi invasion of Kuwait. But the king's position angered his Arab neighbors as well as the United States, leading to a reduction in trade and financial aid from these countries. UN-imposed sanctions (punishing economic measures) on Iraq also led to a huge loss of trade with Iraq. After U.S.-led forces drove Iraqi forces out of Kuwait, the Kuwaiti government expelled about 200,000–300,000 Palestinians from the country. Most of these refugees—many of them skilled and well-off professionals—went to Jordan. Their infusion of money actually brought a boost to the economy during the early 1990s.

Peace agreements—between Israel and the Palestinians in 1993 and between Israel and Jordan in 1994—also provided a temporary boost to Jordan's economy. The newfound stability helped Jordan's tourist industry in particular, as travelers from across the world felt more secure in visiting the region.

But the post-peace-agreement surge was small and short lived. By the end of the 1990s, Jordan's economy was struggling. Burdened by a huge budget deficit, the new king, Abdullah II, sought aid from the World Bank and the International Monetary Fund—organizations that help countries via loans, grants, and financial advice. In 2000 Jordan joined the World Trade Organization, a body that facilitates free trade among members.

By this time, the situation in Iraq had changed in ways that favored Jordan. The UN modified its sanctions program against Iraq to allow the country to sell its oil for food, medicine, and other humanitarian goods. The new arrangement allowed Jordan to purchase oil from Iraq at very low prices. But this agreement came to an abrupt end in early 2003 with the U.S.-led invasion of Iraq and the toppling of Saddam Hussein's regime. The resulting turmoil in Iraq has hurt Jordan's economy. The ongoing violence in Iraq has crippled trade with Jordan. As these difficulties continue, Jordan's economic outlook is difficult to forecast.

In answer to these challenges, King Abdullah II has pushed for programs to make Jordan a Middle Eastern leader in technology. In particular, the Jordanian government is working on programs to increase computer literacy in the country, in hopes of making it the Middle East's hub for information technology (computers, computer networking, Internet services, etc.). By adding the asset of computer literacy to its already well-educated population, the Jordanian government believes the country will be positioned well for the future.

To learn more about King Abdullah II's initiative to make Jordan a hub of information technology in the Middle East, visit www.vgsbooks.com.

 Agriculture

Since Jordan is composed largely of desert, less than 3 percent of Jordan's land is suitable for farming. Just 5 percent of the country's labor force are farmers, and proceeds from agriculture total less than 4 percent of the GDP.

Even Jordan's nondesert areas are susceptible to frequent and severe droughts. To help decrease the damage caused by these rainfall shortages, Jordan invested heavily in irrigation projects in the 1980s. As a result, farming efficiency has increased in recent decades, and much of the country's food products are exported.

Most of Jordan's agricultural activity takes place in the Jordan River valley and in the Jordanian Highlands. The more fertile Jordan River valley produces citrus fruits, melons, and vegetables such as tomatoes and cucumbers. Grains and barley are the main products of the Jordanian Highlands.

Scarce water resources have led the Jordanian government to discourage—and at times ban—the planting of crops that require large amounts of water, such as eggplant and corn.

The country's pastureland is limited and shrinking, due to drought, overgrazing, and desertification. Most livestock—which includes sheep, goats, cattle, and camels—is concentrated in the desert. A large percentage of the country's pastoralists (animal herders) are Bedouin who live the traditional Bedouin lifestyle.

Mining, Manufacturing, and Trade

Although Jordan produces very little oil—the country has only two very small oil wells near the Saudi Arabian and Iraqi borders—it does produce significant amounts of less profitable minerals. These include phosphate and potash, both of which are used in fertilizers. The Dead Sea contains many dissolved minerals, and potash and magnesium are extracted from its waters. Clays, copper ore, and silica (used in the manufacturing of glass and cement) are plentiful.

The export of phosphate contributes a great deal to Jordan's economy, accounting for over 25 percent of export sales. The rock is used in various chemical and industrial processes. The government-owned Jordan Phosphate Mines Company operates mines at Ruseifa near Amman and at al-Hasa and Wadi al-Abyad in the south. A plant on the Dead Sea run by the Arab Potash Company extracts potash from the water by solar evaporation.

Jordan's manufacturing and industrial sector accounts for about 26 percent of GDP and employs 12 percent of the country's workforce. Jordanian manufacturing, which has grown rapidly in recent decades, covers a variety of activities. Most of Jordan's manufacturing income is earned by heavy industry—in particular, phosphate processing, cement production, and oil refining. The country's phosphate extracts are sent to a large chemical fertilizer plant south of Aqaba.

Jordan is one of the Middle East's largest cement producers, with most of this production coming from a large plant located near Amman. Jordan also has one oil refinery near Zarqa, which refines

Mineral salts form on the Dead Sea. Such deposits are valuable resources from which Jordanians mine magnesium and potash.

mostly foreign crude oil. Before the 2003 war in Iraq, most of Jordan's crude oil came from Iraq. Jordan continues to receive oil for refining, but the postwar situation remains unstable. Other sources of crude oil include Saudi Arabia. The oil is transported via the Trans-Arabian Pipeline, which cuts across Jordan's northern desert region.

In recent years, Jordan's government has been pursuing opportunities to exploit the country's large oil shale reserves. Oil shale is a kind of rock from which oil is extracted by distillation. Jordan is believed to have enough oil shale deposits to make the country self-sufficient in oil for several decades.

Light manufacturing makes up the rest of Jordan's manufacturing industry. Jordanian factories produce a wide variety of consumer goods, such as canned fruits and vegetables, olive oil, vegetable fats, batteries, clothing, and other everyday items. Paper, pharmaceutical factories, and several marble works employ thousands of Jordanians. Other full-time industrial activities include milling, oil pressing, bottling and brewing, footwear and furniture manufacturing, glass printing, and canning of cashew nuts and almonds.

Most of Jordan's manufactured goods are created for export. They include clothing, fertilizers, and pharmaceuticals. Jordan also exports large amounts of raw exports, like phosphates, potash, and vegetables. However, Jordan's imports have generally exceeded its exports in value. The most recent estimates available show that imports to Jordan totaled nearly U.S. $5 billion, while exports tallied less than U.S. $3 billion. Part of this deficit is made up by remittances—money sent back to Jordan by Jordanians working abroad.

Jordan's biggest imports are crude oil, fabrics, machinery, transport equipment, and manufactured goods. For the past few decades, Iraq had been Jordan's most important trading partner, but the unrest in Iraq following the 2003 war has threatened this partnership. Jordan's other imports come primarily from Germany, the United States, China, France, Great Britain, and Italy.

Tourism and the Service Sector

Jordan's tourism industry has experienced many ups and downs over the decades, mostly as a result of volatile events in the region. The loss of the West Bank—with its historical and religious towns, such as Jerusalem, Bethlehem, Nablus, and Jericho—in 1967 was a severe blow to Jordanian tourism. The Iraqi invasion of Kuwait in 1990 brought tourism to a virtual halt for an entire year, but the 1994 peace agreement with Israel spurred a record number of tourist visits in 1995. The

1 million or so visitors that year included more than 100,000 Israelis. Tourist stops in Jordan continued to increase throughout the rest of the 1990s, despite the outbreak of violence between Israel and the Palestinians. The negative impact of the 2003 war in Iraq on Jordan's tourism industry has yet to be assessed.

Jordan's Ministry of Tourism and Antiquities promotes the country as an alternative Holy Land, and steps have been taken to preserve historical sites—such as Jerash and Petra—and to develop potentially inviting locations such as the Dead Sea. Most travelers come from the Middle East, although significant numbers of Europeans also make Jordan a destination. In many cases, travelers include a visit to Jordan as part of a journey to several countries in the Middle East.

Little-known attractions of Jordan include the desert castles in the eastern part of the country, most of which were used by the Umayyad caliphs around the eighth century A.D. The caliphs' main residence was in Damascus, but they enjoyed life in the desert and would move with their attendants back to the land where their Bedouin ancestors originated.

People who work in support of Jordan's tourist industry—hotel workers, taxi drivers, tour guides, and others—make up a significant portion of the country's overall service sector. Services are the largest part of Jordan's economy, accounting for more than 70 percent of GDP and employing nearly 83 percent of the country's labor force. Other service-related jobs include the armed forces, government employees, insurers, bankers, and retailers.

Transportation

Jordan has one of the Middle East's better highway systems, and most inland freight is transported by road. Jordan has about 4,500 miles (7,245 km) of paved highways, and the system connects major cities and towns as well as nearby countries. Syria is linked to Jordan via Ramtha, Jerash, and Amman. From the town of Maan, the Desert Highway links the nation with Saudi Arabia. Jordanians can reach the West Bank by a main highway from Amman to Jericho over the Allenby Bridge.

The country's main roadways merge in the southern part of the country and end at Aqaba. Aqaba handles several million tons of cargo annually and is Jordan's only seaport.

Queen Alia International Airport, located about 22 miles (35 km) south of Amman, is the country's main airport, providing service to cities throughout the world. The country's national airline, Royal

As Jordan's only seaport, **Aqaba** is always bustling with activity. The city is also a popular tourist destination.

Jordanian, carries more than 1 million passengers a year, with routes to most Arab lands as well as service to New York, Chicago, and Bangkok, Thailand, and numerous European and African destinations.

Trains still run on the Ottoman-built Hejaz Railway, which passes from the Syrian border through Amman and Maan and on to Saudi Arabia. A connection also links the railway to Aqaba. The entire network spans about 314 miles (505 km) and transports only freight.

The Future

The future makeup of the Middle East remains cloudy, and many vital questions remain unanswered. Will Arabs and Israelis ever find a peaceful resolution to their disputes? Will the Israeli-Palestinian conflict reach a peaceful outcome? Will Palestinian refugees living in Jordan ever be able to return to their homeland? What does the future hold for Iraq after Saddam Hussein? The answers to all of these questions will have a significant impact on Jordan's future. Yet Jordan itself has little control or influence in how these issues are resolved.

However, despite all of this uncertainty, Jordan's future stability appears assured. After more than five years in power, King Abdullah II has shown many of the moderate instincts of his father, while also promoting progress that many hope will brighten the country's financial prospects for the future. Meanwhile, in the relatively short life of the country of Jordan, Jordanian citizens have come to take pride in their country's status as one of the most stable, tolerant, moderate, progressive, and democratic Arab states. If the key Middle Eastern disputes can be resolved and Jordan can stay on its progressive and moderate path, the country seems assured of a bright future.

CA. 8000 B.C. Inhabitants are living in settlements on the banks of the Jordan River.

CA. 2000 B.C. Semitic peoples known as the Amorites begin to move into the region. They soon come to dominate the area, which they name Canaan.

CA. 1300 B.C. The prophet Moses leads the Israelites to Canaan.

CA. 100 B.C. Roman armies conquer the region, naming it Palaestina.

A.D. 400s The Nabataeans, based in their capital of Petra, prosper through trade with other areas of the Middle East.

600s A new religion, Islam, is born in the Arabian Peninsula. Arab people unite to spread this new faith across the Middle East.

661–750 The Sunni Muslim Umayyad dynasty rules the area that later became Jordan.

750 The Abbasids, a new Sunni leadership, conquer the Umayyads and take control of the region.

CA. 1100s Crusaders from western Europe descend on Muslim lands to battle for control of the Holy Land.

1187 Muslim leader Saladin leads his soldiers to victory against the crusaders, effectively ending the Crusades.

1516 Muslim Ottoman Turks annex the area that later became Jordan, as well as Jordan's neighbors, Syria and Palestine, beginning four hundred years of Ottoman rule over the region.

1909 The Young Turks, the new leaders of the Ottoman Empire, call for policies that are objectionable to the Arab people.

1914 Sharif Hussein of the Hejaz is accepted as a spokesperson for the Arab people.

1916 Sharif Hussein launches the Arab Revolt against the Ottoman Turks.

1917 British and Zionist leaders announce the Balfour Declaration, which calls for the creation of a Jewish homeland in Palestine.

1918 Arab forces, fighting alongside the British, defeat the Ottoman Turks.

1920 At a conference in Italy, France and Great Britain divide Syria, Palestine, and the area that later became Jordan among themselves.

1921 British official Winston Churchill draws borders for a British- and French-dominated Middle East. The British place Sharif Hussein's son Abdullah as the ruler of the new nation of Transjordan.

1923   Transjordan declares its independence on May 15, but the British remain in control of many aspects of government.

1930s   Tensions grow in Palestine as more and more Jewish immigrants enter the area.

1948   Jews in Palestine proclaim the State of Israel. Israel's Arab neighbors immediately set out to destroy the new country. Arab Legion forces invade and occupy Jerusalem and the West Bank of the Jordan River. Hundreds of thousands of Palestinian refugees flee to Jordan and settle in UN-run refugee camps.

1950   National elections are held in Jordan. King Abdullah annexes the West Bank and declares the fully independent Hashemite Kingdom of Jordan.

1951   King Abdullah is assassinated in a Jerusalem mosque by a Palestinian nationalist. Abdullah's son Talal is named king.

1952   Talal abdicates due to mental illness. His son, Hussein ibn Talal, is declared king.

1964   Palestinian militants form the Palestine Liberation Organization (PLO). The PLO engages in guerrilla attacks against Israel, often launching their attacks from within Jordan.

1967   Israeli forces crush Jordanian, Egyptian, and Syrian forces during the Six-Day War. The Israelis seize the West Bank. Hundreds of thousands of Palestinians flee to Jordan.

1970   Fighting breaks out between the PLO and the Jordanian Arab Army. Jordanian forces crush the militants. The Palestinian survivors form a group, Black September, that stages a number of sensational terrorist attacks in the following years.

1988   King Hussein abandons Jordan's claim to the West Bank.

1993   Israeli and Palestinian leaders negotiate the Oslo Agreements, which set goals for peace between Israelis and Palestinians.

1994   Jordan signs a peace agreement with Israel.

1999   King Hussein dies on February 7. His son succeeds him as King Abdullah II.

2003   King Abdullah II speaks out against the U.S.-led invasion of Iraq to remove Iraqi president Saddam Hussein.

2004   King Abdullah offers to send Jordanian troops to help in postwar Iraq. The offer is not immediately accepted.

COUNTRY NAME Hashemite Kingdom of Jordan

AREA 35,637 square miles (92,300 sq. km)

MAIN LANDFORMS Jordan Rift Valley, Jordanian Highlands, Jordan Desert

HIGHEST POINT Mount Ramm, 5,689 feet (1,734 m) above sea level

LOWEST POINT Dead Sea, 1,300 feet (400 m)

MAJOR RIVERS Jordan, Yarmuk, Zarqa

ANIMALS jackals, hyenas, foxes, mongooses, wild boars, ibex, hyrax, golden eagles, vultures, pigeons, partridges, scorpions, locusts

CAPITAL CITY Amman

OTHER MAJOR CITIES Irbid, Zarqa, Aqaba

OFFICIAL LANGUAGE Arabic

MONETARY UNIT Jordanian dinar 1000 fils = 1 Jordanian dinar

JORDANIAN CURRENCY

The Jordanian dinar is the currency of the Hashemite Kingdom of Jordan. Also referred to as the "gee-dee," dinar notes are printed in denominations of .500, 1, 5, 10, and 20. The bills have images of past and present Jordanian leaders and Jordanian sites. The Jordanian government also mints 50, 100, 250, 500 fils, and 1 dinar pieces. Each denomination of coin has two different versions of varying size, shape, and color.

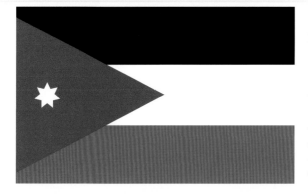

The flag of the Hashemite Kingdom of Jordan was adopted on April 16, 1928. The flag symbolizes the kingdom's roots in the Arab Revolt of 1916 and is adapted from the revolt's banner. The black, white, and green bands represent the Arab Abbasid, Umayyad, and Fatimid dynasties, respectively, while the red triangle that joins the bands represents the Hashemite dynasty. The seven-pointed Islamic star set in the center of the triangle represents the unity of Arab peoples in Jordan.

The Jordanian national anthem, "Long Live the King," was adopted in 1946. The lyrics, written in Arabic by Abdul-Mone'm al-Rifai' praise the kingdom's Hashemite ruler. The anthem's music was composed by Abdul-Qader al-Taneer. Below is an English translation of the anthem.

Long Live the King
Long live the King!
Long live the King!
His position is sublime,
His banners waving in glory supreme.

To find a link where you can listen to Jordan's national anthem, "Long Live the King," as well as view the sheet music for the anthem for a variety of instruments, visit www.vgsbooks.com.

KING ABDULLAH I (1882–1951) The first king of Jordan was born in Mecca, Saudi Arabia. The son of Sharif Hussein, ruler of the Hejaz, Abdullah was educated in Istanbul (in modern-day Turkey). He joined the Arab nationalist movement in 1914 and was a key figure in the Arab Revolt against Ottoman rule during World War I. After the war, the British government backed Abdullah as the leader of the new state of Transjordan. Abdullah supported a moderate approach to the State of Israel. He was assassinated by a Palestinian nationalist in 1951.

KING ABDULLAH II (b. 1962) Born in Amman, King Abdullah II inherited the throne of Jordan when his father King Hussein died in February 1999. After graduating from high school in the United States, Abdullah enrolled at Royal Military Academy Sandhurst in Great Britain. Later, Abdullah joined the Jordanian armed forces. As an officer, he has trained and served in an armored (tank) brigade, as an attack helicopter pilot, and as commander of Jordan's elite Special Forces unit. Since becoming king, Abdullah has sought to continue his father's pro-Western policies. An adventurous personality, Abdullah is a skilled diver, pilot, parachutist, and racecar driver. Like his father before him, he is known to don disguises in order to travel freely through the country to see what conditions are like among his people.

SIR JOHN BAGOT GLUBB (1897–1986) Born in Preston, England, Glubb served as the commander of Jordan's Arab Legion from 1939 to 1956. After serving in the Iraqi government in the late 1920s, Glubb accepted a position as a high-ranking officer in the Arab Legion. In 1931 he formed the Desert Patrol, an elite fighting unit composed entirely of Bedouin fighters. Glubb became overall commander of the Arab Legion in 1939. A trusted friend and adviser of King Abdullah I, Glubb earned the high-ranking title of Glubb Pasha. He led the Arab Legion during the 1948 Arab-Israeli War. In 1956 King Hussein, wishing to cut ties to Jordan's past as a British colony, dismissed Glubb from his position.

KING HUSSEIN (1935–1999) Born in Amman, Hussein reigned as king of Jordan for more than forty-six years. The grandson of King Abdullah I, Hussein assumed the throne at the age of eighteen after his father, King Talal, abdicated due to severe mental illness. Educated in Jordan, Egypt, and Great Britain, Hussein trained for service in the military. Upon taking the throne, he sought to follow in his grandfather's footsteps by encouraging a moderate stance toward Israel that included compromise and negotiation. These views made Hussein controversial in the Arab world. Hussein was a skilled pilot and racecar driver, who enjoyed a variety of hobbies, including skiing, tennis, and diving.

IBRAHIM NASRALLAH (b. 1954) Born in a Palestinian refugee camp in Jordan, Nasrallah is one of the Arab world's better-known poets. Like many writers who have lived and worked in Jordan, Nasrallah is a Palestinian. He has received many awards for his work.

QUEEN NOOR (b. 1951) Born Elizabeth Najeeb Halaby in Washington, D.C., Queen Noor is King Hussein's fourth wife and widow. Born into a wealthy Arab-American family, Halaby earned a degree from Princeton University in New Jersey. In 1977 she went to work for Alia (the airline that later became Royal Jordanian Airlines). Halaby and King Hussein met and married the following year, at which point she adopted the Arabic name Noor and became a Jordanian citizen. As queen she has promoted many causes, including culture and education.

QUEEN RANIA (b. 1970) Queen Rania of Jordan is the wife of King Abdullah II. Born Rania Yassin in Kuwait to a Jordanian family of Palestinian origin, she is one of the most visible first ladies in the Arab world and a champion for women's and children's rights in her country. Rania went to school in Kuwait before earning a degree at the American University in Cairo, Egypt, in 1991. From there she returned to Jordan and worked in the banking industry. Rania met Abdullah in January 1993, and the two were married six months later. In 1995 she established the Jordan River Foundation, an organization designed to help Jordanians increase their productivity and earning power.

MUSTAFA WAHBI AL-TAL (1899–1949) Born in Irbid, al-Tal is Jordan's most famous writer. A lawyer and a judge, he wrote poetry under the pen name 'Arar. His works, which are still widely read in the Middle East, often focused on the idea of Arab nationalism. Al-Tal's hometown holds an annual poetry festival in his honor, and Jordan's most prestigious literary award is named after him.

ABU MUSAB AL-ZARQAWI (b. ca. 1966) According to intelligence and news reports, al-Zarqawi is the leader of a terrorist group that has been blamed for staging suicide bomb attacks, kidnappings, and murders against members of the U.S.-led occupation and against the rebuilding of Iraq. Al-Zarqawi is probably a false name, taken from his birthplace, Zarqa. (Many sources list his real name as Ahmad Fadeel al-Nazal al-Khalayleh.) Al-Zarqawi grew up in a poor family. An angry and violent youth, al-Zarqawi traveled to Afghanistan in the late 1980s to join the jihad (holy war) against the Soviet invasion of that country. Al-Zarqawi returned to Jordan in the early 1990s and was arrested for conspiring to overthrow the Jordanian government. He spent seven years in prison before being released in 1999. Al-Zarqawi is believed to be the mastermind behind a series of kidnappings of civilians in Iraq. U.S. officials have blamed him for a series of videotaped beheadings of these kidnapping victims. The U.S. government has set a $25 million reward for information leading to his capture.

AMMAN Amman has a long and rich history dating back thousands of years. As the capital of the ancient Ammonites, Amman was a small settlement that was an important location during biblical times. It was also a major city (known as Philadelphia) during the era of Roman rule, and its restored six-thousand-seat Roman theater is one of Amman's most popular tourist attractions. Visitors also enjoy exploring the ancient Citadel, a cluster of ruins situated on the highest of Amman's hills. Amman is also home to many mosques, both ancient and modern, as well as museums, art galleries, and a wide variety of markets and shops.

AQABA Jordan's only port is also the country's only seaside resort. Jordanians and other travelers from across the Middle East enjoy swimming, snorkeling, water skiing and other water sports. The city also has a marine aquarium and the Aqaba Fort and Museum. The fort was built in the sixteenth century and was the site of a battle during World War I.

DANA NATURE RESERVE The country's finest nature reserve covers 124 square miles (320 sq. km) in south central Jordan. Hikers can explore a wide variety of landscapes, including sandstone cliffs, sweltering deserts, and semiarid forests, as well as varied plant and animal life. Dana, a small, fifteenth-century village located within the reserve, has been faithfully restored by the Jordanian government and is home to several Bedouin families who are skilled in various Bedouin crafts.

DEAD SEA Each year, tens of thousands of people come from across the globe to float on the surface of the world's saltiest lake. It is virtually impossible to sink in the Dead Sea. At the same time, the water's high salt content causes a person to float so close to the surface that it's almost impossible to perform swimming strokes.

DESERT CASTLES Lying east of Amman within the vast Jordan Desert is a string of desert castles. Historians believe that some of the castles served as desert "vacation homes" for Umayyad officials, where they could entertain guests, feast, and drink in comfort. The largest and most preserved buildings date from the time of the Umayyad dynasty of the seventh and eighth centuries. One of the castles, Qasr (castle) al-Azraq, is famous for its role as a headquarters for British warrior T. E. Lawrence and his Arab allies during the Arab Revolt.

PETRA Each year, hundreds of thousands of tourists travel to this city that was cut out of the walls of a canyon. Historians believe the Treasury, Petra's most famous building, was carved out of the reddish rock between 100 B.C. and A.D. 200. Its imposing 140-foot-high (43 m) facade is probably the country's most photographed site. Petra's theater has a similarly breathtaking facade, but inside this two-thousand-year-old carved-out structure lies a huge theater that once seated up to seven thousand people.

caliph: a successor of Muhammad as the head of Islam

East Banker: generally, a Muslim or Christian native of the area of contemporary Jordan. The term is sometimes used to distinguish native Jordanians from Palestinians living in Jordan.

frontier: a border between two countries

gross domestic product (GDP): a measure of the total value of goods and services produced within a country in a certain amount of time (usually one year). A similar measurement is gross national product (GNP). GDP and GNP are often measured in terms of purchasing power parity (PPP). PPP converts values to international dollars, making it possible to compare how much similar goods and services cost to the residents of different countries.

guerrilla: a person who engages in unconventional warfare, especially as a member of an independent unit carrying out harassment and sabotage

khamsin: a hot desert wind

millet: in the Ottoman Empire, the policy for governance of non-Muslim minorities. The millet system allowed limited self-rule to communities ruled by religious leaders responsible to the central government.

nomad: a member of a people who have no permanent residence but move from place to place, usually seasonally, but within a well-defined territory

Palestinian: generally, a Muslim or Christian native or descendant of the area of Palestine

Quran: the holy book of Islam. The writings of the Quran were set forth by the prophet Muhammad starting in 610. Muslims believe Allah (God) revealed these writings to Muhammad.

refugee: a person forced to flee his or her country due to political upheaval

Sharia: the fundamental law of Islam. The Sharia consists of the Quran and the set of traditions that preserve the conduct and words of the prophet Muhammad.

Shiite: a member of the smaller of the two great divisions of Islam. Shiites supported the claims of Ali (Shiite comes from Shiat Ali, or Party of Ali) and his line as having the right to the Muslim caliphate. On this issue, they are divided with the Sunni.

Sunni: a member of the larger of the two great divisions of Islam. Sunnis supported the traditional method of election to the caliphate and accepted the Umayyad line of caliphs. Over this matter, they conflicted with the Shiite Muslims.

West Bank: the area west of the Jordan River and the Dead Sea, which was annexed by Jordan in 1950 and occupied by Israel in 1967. In July 1988, King Hussein renounced Jordan's claims to the West Bank. A Palestinian government assumed partial authority over the region in the 1990s.

Western: European or North American in outlook, culture, and tradition

Zionism: the international movement for a Jewish homeland in Israel

Glossary

Selected Bibliography

Amin, Mohamed, Duncan Willets, and Sam Kiley. *Journey through Jordan.* **2nd ed. Nairobi: Camerapix Publishers International, 2001.**
This book explores Jordan's rich history and colorful present.

***BBC (British Broadcasting Corporation) News Online.* 2004**
http://news.bbc.co.uk/2/hi/middle_east/default.stm (September 20, 2004).
The BBC News website's Middle East section is a helpful resource for news on Jordan and the Middle East.

Caulfield, Annie. *Kingdom of the Film Stars: Journey into Jordan.* **Oakland: Lonely Planet Publications, 1997.**
Part love story, part travelogue, this memoir by a British writer chronicles her travels to Jordan, where she immerses herself in the country's culture, visits its numerous famous places, and falls in love with a handsome Jordanian tour guide.

Central Intelligence Agency (CIA). *The World Factbook.* **2004.**
http://www.cia.gov/cia/publications/factbook/geos/jo.html (September 20, 2004).
The U.S. government's Central Intelligence Agency maintains *The World Factbook,* which features useful information and statistics on every country in the world, including Jordan.

Dallas, Roland. *King Hussein: A Life on the Edge.* **New York: Fromm International, 1999.**
This biography of King Hussein discusses both his personal and political life and the constant pressures and conflicts he faced throughout his rule.

***The Economist.* 2004.**
http://www.economist.com (September 20, 2004).
Both the website and print edition of this British magazine provide up-to-date coverage of Middle Eastern news.

Ellis, Michael, ed. *Insight Guide: Jordan.* **Singapore: APA Publications, 1999.**
Filled with colorful photos, this book explores the history, people, and culture of Jordan, while highlighting some of the country's best tourist attractions.

Gerner, Deborah J., ed. *Understanding the Contemporary Middle East.* **Boulder, CO: Lynne Rienner Publishers, 2000.**
Covering the Middle East as a whole, this book provides a thorough survey of the people, history, culture, economy, and conflicts of the region.

Greenway, Paul, and Damien Simonis. *Jordan.* **4th ed. Oakland: Lonely Planet Publications, 2000.**
This volume in the Lonely Planet Travel Guide series provides information on Jordan's history, culture, environment, and much more.

Metz, Helen Chapin, ed. *Jordan: A Country Study.* **Washington, DC: Library of Congress, Federal Research Division, 1991.**
http://lcweb2.loc.gov/frd/cs/jotoc.html (September 20, 2004).
This volume in the Library of Congress's Area Handbook series provides an objective analysis of Jordan's history, geography, social systems, economy, and government.

The Middle East and North Africa 2004. London: Europa
Publications Limited, 2004.
This volume in Europa's set of annual surveys features comprehensive essays
about the geography, history, and economy of all the nations of the Middle
East and Africa, including Jordan. Each survey also includes numerous statis-
tics, as well as a lengthy directory of contacts for each country.

Morris, Benny. *The Road to Jerusalem: Glubb Pasha, Palestine, and
the Jews.* **New York: I. B. Tauris, 2002.**
A biography of Glubb Pasha, the British officer who commanded Jordan's Desert
Legion from 1939 to 1956, this book explores the many personalities and conflicts that shaped events in the Middle East during the twentieth century.

Population Reference Bureau. **2004.**
http://www.prb.org (September 20, 2004).
The frequently updated statistics on this site provide a wealth of data on
Jordan's population, birth and death rates, fertility rate, infant mortality rate,
and other useful demographic information.

Rollin, Sue, and Jane Streetly. *Blue Guide: Jordan.* **3rd ed. New York:
W. W. Norton, 2001.**
This travel guide is full of photos and detailed information about sites
throughout Jordan and also includes a chapter about the country's history,
society, and culture.

Tubb, Jonathan B. *Canaanites.* **Norman: University of Oklahoma
Press, 1998.**
A volume in the Peoples of the Past series, this work explores the lives and
culture of the ancient Canaanites, who lived in the area that later became
Jordan, Israel, Lebanon, and Syria.

Weatherby, Joseph N. *The Middle East and North Africa: A Political
Primer.* **New York: Addison Wesley Longman, Inc., 2002.**
This book provides a good background of the Middle East as a whole, includ-
ing Jordan's place and history within the region.

Behnke, Alison, and Vartkes Ehramjian. *Cooking the Middle Eastern Way.* **Minneapolis: Lerner Publications Company, 2005.**
This volume in the Easy Menu Ethnic Cookbooks series features a variety of recipes from countries throughout the Middle East, including Jordan.

Darraj, Susan Muaddi. *Queen Noor.* **Broomall, PA: Chelsea House Publications, 2004.**
This biography of the former queen of Jordan, the widow of King Hussein, chronicles her life with Hussein and her work on behalf of many charitable causes.

Discover Jordan Portal
http://www.discoverjordan.com/directory/kingdom/
This website is loaded with facts about Jordan's history, monarchy, people, culture, geography, and economy.

Finkelstein, Norman. *Ariel Sharon.* **Minneapolis: Lerner Publications Company, 2005.**
This biography explores the early life, military, and political career of the controversial prime minister of Israel and how his actions and policies have helped to shape the Middle East.

Headlam, George. *Yasser Arafat.* **Minneapolis: Lerner Publications Company, 2004.**
This biography follows the life and career of the controversial Palestinian militant leader, whose aims often clashed with those of King Hussein of Jordan.

Katz, Samuel M. *Global Counterstrike: International Counterterrorism.* **Minneapolis: Lerner Publications Company, 2005.**
This volume in Lerner's Terrorist Dossiers series profiles some of the world's best counterterrorist teams, including Jordan's elite counterterrorist brigade, CTB-71.

____. *Jerusalem or Death: Palestinian Terrorism.* **Minneapolis: Lerner Publications Company, 2003.**
One of the volumes in Lerner's Terrorist Dossiers series, this book explores the origins, history, and goals of Palestinian terrorism.

Losleben, Elizabeth. *The Bedouin of the Middle East.* **Minneapolis: Lerner Publications Company, 2003.**
Learn more about the culture and daily lives of the Bedouin people, one of Jordan's largest ethnic groups.

PBS: *Islam: Empire of Faith*
http://www.pbs.org/empires/islam/
This is the companion website to the three-part PBS film on the ancient Islamic Empire, *Islam: Empire of Faith.* The site features essays from the film's producers, a comprehensive timeline of events, and profiles of important Muslim leaders.

Schneider, Mical. *Between the Dragon and the Eagle.* **Minneapolis: Carolrhoda Books, 1996.**
This story follows a bolt of silk as it travels the trade route between China and Rome, including a stay in Petra among the Nabataeans.

Further Reading and Websites

Sherman, Josepha. *Your Travel Guide to Ancient Israel.*
Minneapolis: Lerner Publications Company, 2004.
Learn more about the lives and customs of the people of ancient Israel, an area
that encompassed much of western Jordan.

Slavik, Diane, and Ray Webb. *Daily Life in Ancient and Modern
Jerusalem.* **Minneapolis: Runestone Press, 2001.**
Through colorful illustrations and vivid photographs, this book follows the history
of Jerusalem—once a part of Jordan—from ancient times to the present.

vgsbooks.com
http://www.vgsbooks.com
Visit vgsbooks.com, the homepage of the Visual Geography Series®. You can
get linked to all sorts of useful on-line information, including geographical,
historical, demographic, cultural, and economic websites. The vgsbooks.com
site is a great resource for late-breaking news and statistics.

Wagner, Heather Lehr. *Gertrude Bell: Explorer of the Middle East.*
Broomall, PA: Chelsea House Publications, 2004.
A biography for young readers, this book explores the fascinating life of
Gertrude Bell, a British citizen who traveled to the Middle East in the early
twentieth century, wrote several books about her travels, and had a major
impact on events in the region.

Zwier, Lawrence J., and Matthew S. Weltig. *The Persian Gulf and
Iraqi Wars.* **Minneapolis: Lerner Publications Company, 2005.**
This book explores the origins, events, and outcomes of the two U.S.-led wars
against Jordan's neighbor, Iraq.

Captions for photos appearing on cover and chapter openers:

Cover: Hadrian's Arch, also known as the Triumphal Arch, marks the southern entrance to the city of Jerash. The arch was built to honor the Roman emperor Hadrian's visit to the historic city in A.D. 129.

pp. 4–5 At 1,300 feet (400 m) below sea level, the Dead Sea is the lowest point on the earth and is too salty to sustain any plant or animal life. Known for its healing properties, the sea is popular with tourists and locals alike.

pp. 8–9 The sandstone mountains of Wadi Rum rise majestically from the desert floor. The area is perhaps best known as the area T. E. Lawrence was based in during the Arab Revolt (1916–1918). Much of the 1962 film *Lawrence of Arabia* was filmed in Wadi Rum.

pp. 20–21 This Byzantine-era mosaic map of the Holy Land and surrounding area is one of the treasures of the city of Madaba. Included on the map are the Jordan River, the Dead Sea, and the town of Jericho. The original map is thought to have been made of more than 2.3 million tiles and measured 16 by 82 feet (5 by 25 m).

pp. 38–39 Men wearing kaffiyehs (cloth headdresses commonly worn by Arab men) enjoy a chat together. Arabs account for 98 percent of Jordan's population.

pp. 46–47 A Muslim man studies the Quran, the Islamic holy book. Most of Jordan's population practices Islam, and religion is an important aspect of everyday life.

pp. 58–59 The official currency of Jordan is the dinar.

Photo Acknowledgments

The images in this book are used with the permission of: © John Elk III, pp. 4–5, 10; © Nevada Wier, pp. 8–9; © Richard T. Nowitz/CORBIS, p. 13; © Steve Kaufman/CORBIS, p. 14 (left); © Trip/M. Peters, p. 14 (right); © Alison Wright/Panos Pictures, pp. 16–17, 57 (bottom); © Wolfgang Kaehler/CORBIS, p. 18; © Yann Arthus-Bertrand/CORBIS, p. 19; © Art Directors/Trip/Helene Rodgers, pp. 20–21, 24–25; © Erich Lessing/Art Resource, p. 22; © Library of Congress (LC-matpc-05807), p. 27; © Bettmann/CORBIS, p. 31; © Reuters/CORBIS, pp. 34, 37; © Annie Griffiths Belt/CORBIS, pp. 38–39; © Ali Jarekji/Reuters/CORBIS, pp. 40, 54; Glacomo Pirozzi/Panos Pictures, p. 43; © Trip/A. Ghazzal, pp. 46–47; © Francoise de Mulder/CORBIS, p. 48; © Trip/H. Rogers, pp. 52, 58–59; © Nader/CORBIS SYGMA, pp. 53, 57 (top); © Jean-Leo Dugasi/Panos Pictures, p. 62; © Ben Mangor/SuperStock, p. 65; © www.banknotes.com, p. 68.

Cover photo: John Kruel/Independent Picture Service. Back cover: NASA.